PERSEVERE:
Journey with Jordan

By Debbie Willis

With a foreword by Dr. Casey Treat

Dedication

With love to my ever-patient and loving
husband, Paul, who lives this
adventure with me,
and to my living children, Blake and Morgan,
who bring such joy to my life.
I love you beyond measure.

Foreword

I remember the day Debbie called me and told me her newborn son, Jordan, was very sick and may be so for some time. I felt sad, mad, and challenged because one of my friends and a leader of our ministry was being attacked by the enemy; it was not right. I told the Lord it was not right; I bound the devil, loosed the angels of God, and did everything I knew to do to help Jordan be healed. Debbie and her husband, Paul, helped to start Christian Faith Center. They gave and served as elders and staff members. They were (and are) serious Christians who really were living the Word of God. How could this be happening to them?

Debbie and Paul Willis are two of the heroes in my life. This story will make a difference in your life. In spite of the challenges they have faced as parents of a developmentally disabled child, they are happy, generous, and positive servants of the Lord and His Church, who have raised godly children. They have refused to be victims of this circumstance, or be angry at God because of their pain. I suppose most people would see them as successful business and church leaders who never have had a problem. They never whine or complain, and have more time to help than most.

As a young man, Jordan was still dealing with medical, mental and physical disabilities. He was a great guy, but Satan came to steal, kill, and destroy part of his life. Daily, this family faced sickness, accidents, and needs to which I can only try to relate. Yet, they stood and continued to stand on God's Word and live prosperous lives. They are examples to us all of what we can be if we are willing to walk with God in every circumstance. Their story will inspire and encourage you to overcome the problems you may be facing.

I don't think Jordan knew he had a problem. He was loved, taught, and challenged to be all he could be every day. Just like you and me, he lived to his utmost, and had good days and bad days. I prayed he would be healed and whole before he got to Heaven. That didn't happen, but Jordan will be waiting to greet us when we arrive. Either way, he and his family are overcomers. They overcame every challenge and every negative because they have chosen to walk with God and believe His Word, rather than submit to this world.

Their story will help you face your challenges and overcome your problems. Ours may seem small in comparison, or maybe even worse, but we can still win. Whiners are never winners — but through Christ we can overcome — the Willis family will show you how to win.

Dr. Casey Treat| Founder and Senior Pastor
Christian Faith Center| Federal Way, WA

Table of Contents

Prelude

While sipping cappuccino on a beautiful morning in a small, ancient cliff town in Italy, the first day of a family vacation, suddenly, my heart clenched. I gasped for air and remembered the date...March 18th, 2011, the first anniversary of my beloved son, Jordan's death, exactly one year ago.

Not a day went by when I could escape from his memory. Every day brought a reminder; every Monday, I remembered Jordan's breathing tube being removed, and how happy he became; Tuesday, playing butterfly kisses and little finger games with him, as I watched and heard the machines buzz with respiratory information; Wednesday, when we made that final, impossible, gut-wrenching decision to allow our sweet boy to die; Thursday, when he took his final ride home; Friday, the day of his last shallow breath. I remember him every morning as I wake up and every night before falling asleep. Yes, indeed, I remember. I remember, and my heart grips in pain.

On that particular morning, being distracted by a new time zone and unfamiliar environment,

I actually forgot. I was with my husband and mother, on the first day of our long-planned Italian vacation, celebrating my mother's 80th birthday. As my eyes welled up and the tears began to flow, I thought, *OK, now Debbie, you have a choice. Remember? It is the choice you have made every day for a year. You can choose to make it a good day or a sad day. Jordan is fine, more than fine. You are in a lovely place. You are in Italy on vacation. We are all going to have fun. Do not allow your grief to ruin this day, this vacation, your life. Keep breathing. Keep moving forward.* All three of us paused a moment... a quiet, bittersweet moment. I sighed, wiped my tears away, and said, "Let's make this a good day."

For the 25 years of Jordan's life, the success of our family was made by decisions – daily, sometimes hourly, decisions based on God's Word and our faith in it. Our family values are what God directed in the Bible. God is the foundation of our lives, the source of every good thing and the answer to our needs. Without Him, there would be no success, no happy family. Without Him, there would be disastrous calamity.

I want my son's life to serve a purpose. I want to share with you how our whole family not only survived, but thrived during the 25 years of Jordan's life. I will offer you the truth; my raw emotions are not edited. You will learn the good, the bad and the ugly (I can be ugly).

I have found there is very little written, especially from a Christian perspective, about how a family can live successfully through the challenges of a special needs child. Most of our friends could sympathize and support, but had no practical experience. I am not a doctor or counselor. I am a mother who had a huge responsibility dumped on my lap — sink or swim.

Why are you reading this? Do you have a disabled child or maybe there is some other challenge with which you are dealing? Whatever your need is, my earnest prayer is that you will glean tools to enable you to handle your difficult situation better. God's Word is true and can be applied to anyone for anything. You have everything to gain!

Chapter 1
JORDAN

As I slowly emerged from anesthesia, following a grueling 40 hour labor that culminated in a cesarean, I asked for my baby. I heard, "Mrs. Willis, your baby is very sick." As those words registered in my foggy brain, my eyes popped open, and giving no regard to my very recent incision, I bolted from my bed. Shoving me back, restrained by several healthcare workers and sedated again, I fought sleep, desperate to comprehend what those words meant. It was the morning of January 28, 1986.

My husband, Paul, having been told I would be in recovery for some time and then sleep, left to go home. He saw the baby being carried to intensive care to keep a close eye on him due to the long labor. Upset about how the delivery went, but not aware of any great cause for concern, he left. During the entire intensive labor and cesarean delivery, he could not sleep and was exhausted; certainly not more tired than I, but still very spent. On his way home, Paul stopped by our church looking for a hug; nothing went as we planned. One of our friends saw him from a window, and they met in the parking lot. With tears in his eyes, Paul gave the report of our experience, still not knowing how bad it really was.

When I slowly awakened in my hospital room and became aware, I urgently began asking for my baby. Several doctors came to my room looking grim to tell me my newborn son, whom we named, Jordan, experienced a significant hemorrhage in the brain, a stroke at birth. They did not know if he could see or hear, or if he would ever walk. They did, however, know he developed a seizure disorder. I tried to absorb what I had been told, but it was hard to focus. I felt fear grip my heart. I cried out in disbelief. What did this mean? It was hard to comprehend. I asked what I did wrong? They assured me there was nothing. I was in shock and heartbroken.

Immediately, I called Paul, and through tears, the words spilled out. I'm not sure how much he could comprehend of my muffled, choking words, I could not speak clearly, but he got the gist. Enraged with the doctors, he could not mentally grasp why they let him leave knowing there were problems with his newborn; furious at not being present with his wife while she learned something so devastating.

That very day we began physical therapy on Jordan. I was taught how to handle him, how to position him, how to medicate him. Many things that, frankly, I did not want to learn. I did not want to accept that my child had special needs. I felt angry, even furious, as I learned a new language of medical terms, and heard what doctors said to expect. I did not want to know all of this.

Jordan and I spent quite a lot of time together in the hospital learning to nurse. Due to the stroke, Jordan could not easily make his mouth form correctly to enable him to suck successfully. When he mastered that task, we left the hospital with these words of wisdom: take him home and love him. I knew loving him would not be difficult, because he had already captured my heart, but I understood what the nurse meant, love him enough to accept him and do whatever necessary to bring out the very best in him. Thus, began our journey with Jordan.

We arrived home and there we sat, Jordan, Paul, and me. Paul and I hardly knew what to do with a baby, let alone one with special needs. We all know that children do not come with a specific manual of how to care for and raise them, but surprisingly they just let us take this sick baby home, like a normal child, and expected us to care for him. I was afraid. Can we do this? We hardly knew how to change his diapers. We knew the seizure disorder required medication. We knew he would need physical therapy to help him regain strength in the weak areas from the stroke, but what else? What would our lives become? How was this going to work out?

OVERCOMING THE SHOCK

The shock you experience is overwhelming when you learn your child has tremendous special needs. The shock gives way to anger and then sadness — a pattern somewhat similar to what would be experienced when a loved one dies. The difference is that with death, you acknowledge the loss, and move on — maybe slowly — but time lessens the sadness and even though you never forget, eventually, for the most part, you heal. There are differences with a severely developmentally disabled child. Paul and I never could put the experience behind us. Jordan became a living, breathing, daily reminder of what we, and he, lost. Looking at him, we would always feel the sadness of what should have been. What would his gifts and talents have been? What would he have accomplished? What would his personality have been? Who would his friends have been? Who would he have married? How many children would he have had? So many questions without answers, so I went to the Word of God.

While babies do not come with a manual, we had THE manual, the Bible, the greatest, most important book ever written. With our new need in our lives, the Bible became alive to us with information we did not *see* before. My Bible became my friend in a whole new way. I hadn't planned for this, a sick child. I did not want to deal with it. Still in shock, I needed help. Yes, I already knew a lot of what the Word said, but with this new extraordinary challenge I read with new eyes. The Bible is not a long set of rules of do's and don'ts. While it contains history, it is not just words. We not only have to read with our eyes but also with our spirit. The Bible is alive. God is the One and only solution that will bring us the results we need. He does not save us from all difficulty in life, but He does save us from defeat. Life can be challenging, and we sometimes find ourselves in situations with our children, marriage, parents, health, employment, or other circumstances, and we don't know what to do. These situations can be the result of choices we made or something beyond our control. Regardless of what your situation is, there is One answer: the Holy One, the King of kings, and Lord of lords. You can overcome!

Regardless of how our challenges come about, our lives are forever changed. It is how we handle them that will determine the course of our future. While we never stop living by faith, there comes a time when we must decide how we're going to live in the here and now. How would we avoid becoming another statistic — *victims of circumstance* — and start to overcome? The answer is surprisingly simple, but not necessarily easy: step by step, day by day, decision by decision, with a boat-load of prayer. We listened for the unction of the Holy Spirit.

We wanted to hear His voice, and we wanted to walk in an attitude of love and wisdom. We did not know much of anything experientially because we never walked this path before. We walked by faith.

MOVING ON

Determined we would live our lives as normally as possible, we discovered a new kind of normal. Life had changed, certainly, but we would not allow ourselves to become morose. We had a business to run, our work in the ministry, our marriage, our lives. We faced tremendous challenges and hard decisions, but if we gave up on our calling, our future, essentially, it would allow the devil to steal even more from us.

Jordan's needs went well beyond our, or any of our friends', experience. Great support, but little practical advice. Even with God, in a sense, we forged our own trail. Had we known everything that would occur in our future as the years went by; well, I am glad I didn't.

We loved our boy; charming and oh so cute, but as time went by we knew Jordan was also profoundly mentally and physically handicapped. Much of what the doctors predicted at birth came to pass. Subsequent brain surgery caused further damage. As an adult, Jordan functioned at the level of a two-year-old at best. Considered medically fragile, with his health carefully monitored every day, he needed around-the-clock care. We watched him every waking moment and monitored him frequently at night. Sleep was often elusive.

From what I learned, having a developmentally disabled child causes more stress in a family than the death of a spouse. Though I cannot verify that statement, I can tell you it was devastating. Always in front of us, our care of him would never stop. We believed he would outlive us, so we needed to prepare for his life beyond us. For as long as he lived, for as long as we lived, he would need constant supervision and monitoring of all aspects of his life. Institutionalizing Jordan being an option, we knew that was not what we wanted for him. The decision to keep Jordan at home was not difficult to make, but living with the decision became very challenging. The result was worth the effort. Jordan became a sweet boy who knew nothing but love.

Jordan received the best care possible, including that of alternative healthcare professionals, which I will discuss later, and eventually, a caregiver who came to love him as much as we did. His development exceeded his prognosis. Jordan's pediatrician and neurologist consistently expressed surprise at his development. One time, the word *amazing* came out of his neurologist's mouth.

We experienced many, many challenges raising Jordan, but one thing is sure, Jordan was a happy camper, always treated with dignity and love. His smile was the world's greatest. Jordan didn't know he had a problem. As long as people cared for him, having his books, videos, puzzles, and tortilla chips, he was happy. He loved to snuggle and get butterfly kisses. He loved music and being around people; a very social guy. Being social, he liked to touch people and get their attention. As much as possible, we kept Jordan clean and well-dressed, aware that it would be hard for some people to get past his obvious disabilities. We made sure that the things over which we could control, primarily personal hygiene and clean clothing, became high priority.

Jordan liked to be included in everything. It surely tested the patience of his brother and sister. When our younger children, Blake and Morgan, invited friends over, playing games on the floor, if Jordan didn't get the attention he considered due him, he would lie on the floor and mess up the game. I would hear, "JORDAN!" followed by his chuckle, and I knew what happened. The children would distract him with another activity. I tried to allow them to resolve these challenges on their own. For the most part, the kids exercised patience with him. Sometimes I needed to intervene when he became very intent on being a pest.

As a youngster, I could physically handle Jordan on my own. I took him everywhere. He was never hidden. When our other tots arrived, we all went together. As Jordan grew, I needed another adult with me to help. Sometimes it would be his caregiver, and frequently it would be our very generous friend, Terry Schurman, who became Aunt T to my children. We would load the van with all our children and off we would go for some fun adventure. Fridays were usually our play day; we called it Adventure Friday.

Occasionally, Paul and I took Jordan on family trips. On one trip, we took him to Disneyland. Wow, what a complete blast! For the first time ever in our other children's minds, Jordan became a great asset. His disabilities enabled us to get to the front of the lines faster. We went on roller coasters, time after time after time; it was his favorite thing to do at an amusement park, loving the feeling in his tummy.

One of Jordan's great passions was horseback riding, called hippotherapy. He didn't know it as a form of physical therapy. He just loved being on the horse. I would say, "We are going to ride your horse today, Jordan," and he would become terribly excited. Often he knew exactly what was going on. His infrequent normal responses thrilled me!

ESCAPE ARTIST

Jordan loved attending church, especially during praise and worship. He did his own version of dancing. He held onto the chair in front of him and pumped his legs up and down, chuckling and making excited noises; very cute to watch. He got a little antsy during the sermon and would sometimes grunt his impatience. Once, in Children's Church, somehow he escaped, and ran into the front of the sanctuary during the service, right past the pulpit. Our pastor, Casey Treat, said, *Hi, Jordan*, and kept on preaching. Upset, the staff and volunteers in the children's ministry could not believe they lost track him. Extremely mortifying was when Jordan pulled the emergency handle in a hall at church that called the fire department. That red pull was too hard to resist. I hustled him to the car and watched as the fire trucks arrived. The trucks roared by me with the culprit sitting so innocently in the car. This happened twice!

One day, Jordan escaped from our yard. We could not find him anywhere. We were horrified, and ready to call the police; he did not have on his helmet to protect his head and face should he fall during a seizure. I knew he would not go into the woods because of instability. He must be somewhere in the neighborhood, unless he had been kidnapped. I kind of chuckled at that, because at that time Jordan looked quite normal other than walking with a limp. It would take a few minutes for a kidnapper to figure out that he had snatched someone with developmental problems. I considered asking the kidnappers for ransom to take Jordan back.

We began a neighborhood search. Walking was part of Jordan's physical therapy, so Paul started his route. He found him trotting up the road with one of our good friends and neighbor, Wendy Treat. The lady from a neighboring house said she found Jordan sitting on her kitchen floor, eating fresh chocolate chip cookies. Having no idea where he belonged, she headed to a house frequently populated with a boatload of kids in the yard – the Treats'.

Another time, escaping the yard, we found him in another neighbor's house. While eating dinner, they heard their piano being played. By this time, everyone knew Jordan and where he lived. Shortly thereafter, we installed an electric gate across the driveway and fencing around the yard to keep him safe. Most kids eventually learn the skill of self-preservation; Jordan never fully developed that ability.

SCHOOLS

At three, Jordan qualified for early education in the public school system, a pre-school program for developmentally disabled children. At the time, he was referred to as *developmentally delayed*, as though he would catch up at some point, and early intervention was believed to help. I wrote about all his deficits to make my case that he needed early intervention education; this was very challenging, in that our confession was for Jordan's healing. When accepted, the school staff and I developed a document called an Adaptive Education Plan (AEP), a legally binding contract listing what they would do for Jordan. They wrote goals for physical and occupational therapy, language development, behavior issues, potty training, and others. What Jordan became thrilled about was the bus! A little school bus picked him up at our home and delivered him back a few hours later. Jordan knew what the words *school* and *bus* meant. He loved it.

Although I think Jordan received some benefit from his early education, the entire school process became challenging. I found I needed to advocate for Jordan as the exercises on his AEP were not accurately followed, due to unrealistic goals and lack of staff. I think the teachers and administrators believed they knew more about Jordan than I did. I respectfully, and sometimes not so respectfully, disagreed with those in authority, sometimes leading to outright shouting matches.

Advocate, advocate, advocate for your child or your loved one whose needs are not being addressed. Vulnerable people need an advocate, someone who will take responsibility to see that they are safe, cared for, and however possible, socialized. The desire for socialization is normal, and with rare exception, essential for quality of life. Without someone to advocate for a vulnerable or incapacitated person, and no one person is accountable, there is room for abuse.

At one time, Jordan was potty trained, but after numerous and lengthy hospitalizations, he lost that ability, making it fairly impossible for him to *go* on demand. In other words, he did not perceive the urge. Jordan would be taken to the bathroom at specific times of day, would be unable to urinate, but on the way back to class sometimes wet his pants (he wore disposable underwear, so he usually did not soil his clothing). A school psychologist believed him to be deliberate, exhibiting bad, purposeful, behavior. Had I not intervened, advocating for my son, Jordan's reputation, and perhaps his treatment, could have been compromised. The psychologist could not understand it to be a medical issue. I pretty much came unglued on her.

One thing that might have made it easier for Jordan to have success would have been a bathroom within the classroom, designated for that room's use. The school did not have one. Every other school Jordan attended contained this resource. The school recently went through a retrofit, and still did not have a bathroom installed in the disabled classroom. I started writing to the school board, the city council and anyone else I could think of. Apparently, formal meetings on the topic took place to which I did not receive an invitation but eventually I learned that during the following summer a designated bathroom would be built. Jordan aged out of the public school system and did not benefit from it, but due to my advocacy, kids today are benefitting from that much needed resource. Even though the school *officially* was not real pleased with me, the teachers privately expressed their thanks and appreciation.

Once, I got a call from the school nurse. She said she found what appeared to be mostly healed marks on Jordan's right thigh. They looked like cigarette burn marks. I told her that no one smoked in our family, and I would check him when he got home. She said she would be following up with her concern. Her tone led me to believe she suspected child abuse. When he got home, we headed to the bathroom. Some of Jordan's behaviors could be odd, like using a finger to poke on his thigh, bruising himself. That is what the school nurse saw. Fortunately, it ended there, with no repercussions. Alarmed, I totally appreciated her advocacy on Jordan's behalf.

We put a notebook in Jordan's school backpack that also contained a change of clothing and disposable underwear. Every day the school staff and our family communicated with each other via the notebook with anything specific we felt the other needed to know. When Jordan's seizures left him pretty beaten up, I wrote detailed explanations. Those fading bruises on his leg were worthy of a call from the school nurse, but I never received a call regarding his bruised, black and blue face, and broken teeth.

DEALING WITH THE GOVERNMENT

When Jordan turned 18, legally he would become an adult. Our legal ability to make decisions on his behalf would stop. To be able to continue to care for him, we needed to apply for guardianship of our own child. To do that, we needed to have him declared legally incapacitated, at which time Jordan would become a ward of the State of Washington. The State would have legal authority over him, not us. I was both stunned and appalled. Who would love and care for him like we did?

First, we said, why bother with all the legal stuff? Who is standing behind us waiting to take oversight of a medically fragile, mentally and physically disabled adult? Surprisingly there are plenty, and that was not happening on our watch. Guardianship is big business. Companies get money from the State to care for incapacitated people. The government tries to oversee the spending of these funds, as well as the person's care, but in reality, the government cannot possibly monitor everything.

We applied to be the guardians of our son. It was a long, laborious process. We hired an attorney; Jordan, had one, too, appointed by the State and paid for using our tax dollars. I filled out copious quantities of legal documents. During a visit to our home, Jordan's attorney asked him if he wanted his parents to keep taking care of him. Clueless, but being clean, with a well cared for appearance, we and our home passed inspection. Who could not be impressed with Jordan's bright red car bed, right? Appearing in court, a judge who reviewed our application approved us for three years as his legal guardians, the longest term allowed by Washington State law. What an invasive ordeal. It could have been worse; some people are only appointed for one year. Towards the end of the three-year period, another round of documents would need to be submitted for approval, as well as another appearance before a judge. If too much time elapsed, there existed a possibility that we could lose the privilege of guardianship. Honestly, the experience — un-fun, a little intimidating, and expensive. We completed tons of documents to get guardianship— tons of documents every three years to keep him, and tons of documents when he died, every time, appearing before a judge.

I feel sorry for incapacitated people who do not have family or loving friends to care for them. For us, there was never a question that Jordan would continue to live at home as an adult under our careful watch.

On a side note, I have to say it stunned me the amount of paperwork involved. It is necessary because so many people do not have integrity. As a result, the legal system assumes the worst case scenario, until proven wrong. People do a lot of dishonest, evil, harmful things to those who are vulnerable, thus the lengthy, full-of-suspicion, process. Anything that hurts the mentally disabled, elderly, or children infuriates me.

As a young child, at first glance, Jordan looked normal, a very handsome child, with brightness in his eyes and a winning smile. His daddy sometimes called him *Sparkles*. I called him a *handsome-hunk-of-stuff*. I often thought, *good thing you are so cute to look at, because you are a lot of work*. Of course, he did not know what I said or what it meant, but since I smiled, he beamed at me. I know all parents think their babies are cute, and they are. It was very hard to realize that this beautiful, normal looking child could have so many problems. He greeted me every time I got him out of his crib in the morning with a bright and shining smile. When we went out in public with him, people began to comment on his beautiful appearance. It made his father and me smile. If the seizures had not taken their toll and his brain surgery, which I will talk about later, had not stunted his growth, he would have been well over 6' tall with thick, dark hair, beautiful eyes, and a killer smile; think JFK, Jr. It is bittersweet to enjoy the memory of his handsome looks. What should have been that would never be.

Chapter 2
PERSPECTIVE

I have been asked dozens of times about how we managed. Sometimes I thought *beats me*, or *did I have an option?* I must have gone through the wrong door on my way to motherhood. People offered their sincere compliments, but I believe inside they praised God it skipped them. I understand that thinking. As awful as it may sound, I wish it had not happened to my family either.

Blake has said, "Jordan was really blessed to be born into our family, because we gave him a good life." Blake's perspective is better. Do not blame God for your troubles. He is not the problem. He is the answer. You have to choose to have the proper perspective for your situation.

Here is an excellent example of perspective, said in the best way I have ever heard:

WELCOME TO HOLLAND
By Emily Perl Kingsley

I am often asked to describe the experience of raising a child with a disability — to try to help people who have not shared that unique experience to understand it, to imagine how it would feel. It's like this....

When you're going to have a baby, it's like planning a fabulous vacation trip — to Italy. You buy a bunch of guidebooks and make your wonderful plans. The Coliseum. The Michelangelo David. The gondolas in Venice. You may learn some handy phrases in Italian. It's all very exciting.

After months of eager anticipation, the day finally arrives. You pack your bags and off you go. Several hours later, the plane lands. The flight attendant comes and says, "Welcome to Holland."

"Holland?!" you say. "What do you mean, Holland?? I signed up for Italy! I'm supposed to be in Italy. All my life I've dreamed of going to Italy."

But there's been a change in the flight plan. They've landed in Holland, and there you must stay.

The important thing is, they haven't taken you to a horrible, disgusting, filthy place full of pestilence, famine and disease. It's just a different place.

So you must go out and buy new guidebooks. You must learn a whole new language. And you'll meet a whole new group of people you would never have met.

It's just a different place. It's slower-paced than Italy, less flashy than Italy. But after you've been there for a while, and you catch your breath, you look around... And you begin to notice that Holland has windmills... Holland has tulips. Holland even has Rembrandt's. But everyone you know is busy coming and going from Italy... And they're bragging about what a wonderful time they had there. And for the rest of your life you will say, "Yes, that's where I was supposed to go. That's what I had planned."

And the pain of that will never, ever, ever, ever go away... because the loss of the dream is a very, very significant loss.

But... If you spend your life mourning the fact that you didn't get to Italy, you may never be free to enjoy the very special, very lovely things... about Holland.

Here are a few more examples of perspective. As he grew, Jordan's teeth took an awful beating during falls from his seizures. Although we tried to protect his mouth with a face guard attached to a helmet that protected him from head trauma, during seizures sometimes his mouth and teeth still got injured. One time after a fall I expected him to be fine. His helmet on, he fell on the grass, but when I looked at him, I saw two badly chipped front teeth. Terribly upset, I cried and cried, feeling bad even the next day. It was grievous to me. We had worked so hard to protect those teeth. I told my neighbor, friend, boss, and pastor, Casey Treat, what happened. He responded with, "Wow, it could have been his head that got broken." I felt pulled up by my boot-straps, and I began to praise God. It is all about perspective.

One time Paul and I went to a movie. At that time Jordan was 21. We did not leave our 15-year-old daughter, Morgan, alone with Jordan very often. Due to his size, she had difficulty controlling him physically. If he did not want to do something, he did not have enough respect for her authority to comply. He would just laugh at her when she got frustrated. I can still hear his chuckle. Physically, too big for me as well, he usually respected my authority as his mother enough to comply.

Another reason we did not leave him alone with Morgan often is because he could soil his diaper and need a change. Again, physically it was challenging to get him to comply. Not real appropriate, you might think, having a young lady changing a man's diaper. Lots of those kinds of situations occurred; our family just learned to deal with them.

As I explained earlier, Jordan was totally potty trained at one time, but all the hospitalization stays caused some desensitizing to take place from the use of a catheter, and during frequent hospital stays, he couldn't get out of bed for bowel movements. He simply lost his ability to use the toilet.

On this particular occasion, Jordan was changed just before we departed for the movie. Since we would only be gone a little over 2 hours, we believed it would be safe. We told Morgan the movie we would see, at what theater, our cell phone numbers already in her phone.

Sometime during the movie, my phone began to vibrate. When I left the theater, I saw numerous calls from Morgan. I didn't feel them. I called her and could tell from the background noise she was not at home. I asked what she needed, dreading her response; she said Jordan soiled his diaper, and she could not get him to cooperate to change him. I asked her location, she told me she was on the freeway in Dad's car driving to find us since we did not respond to her calls. At 15, Morgan was not a licensed driver, and had very little experience. I began to panic. I asked where Jordan was? At home locked in the bathroom, she replied. I began to panic more. As calmly as possible I told Morgan to get off the freeway, get onto side streets, go home and drive slowly. Paul and I ran out of the theater and drove home like crazy people, which, at the moment, was an accurate description. We arrived home before our daughter.

On the way, I wondered aloud how Morgan locked Jordan in the bathroom? I envisioned rope around the outer bathroom door handle and then attached to the piano leg. In reality, she locked the bathroom door from the inside, meaning we would be locked out, but Jordan could exit the bathroom at will — and, that's exactly what he did.

The odor of feces assaulted us when we opened

the door. Jordan was sitting on the family room sofa (leather, we learned not to have fabric long before), happy as can be. Covered from head to toes, he left poopy shoe track marks on the carpet, and finger painting in the hall. The toilet, sink, floors and walls in the bathroom defied description. Hair, face, everything was covered. I have no idea how he could have spread the stuff so far.

I raced upstairs to start bathwater in another bathroom as my husband gingerly removed Jordan's shoes and carried him up the stairs. Paul plopped him into the tub, clothes and all. When Morgan arrived home, we made her sit with him to keep Jordan safe in the tub while we cleaned up the mess. Filling the tub twice because the water turned cold, Jordan was a prune. Our daughter began to complain that she was getting bored, and we lovingly yelled, "TOUGH!" When I recounted this saga to a friend, she laughed so hard and long that she cried. Horrified with the situation, I did not see the humor. When I saw it from her perspective, I laughed, too.

REACH OUT

There are reasons that God told us to assemble ourselves together (Hebrews 10:25). Many times, Paul and I have felt frustrated, angry, and every other emotion you can imagine. We cannot always counsel each other because we are often experiencing the same emotions and challenges.

It has been our friends who have helped us put thoughts back into perspective. It is helpful to tell a trusted friend about something particularly challenging. It cleans you out. I did not want to be a person who griped and complained all the time, but in our challenging lives, we needed an outlet. I didn't discuss these challenges with bunches of people, because speaking a problem is not how we walk in faith, but sometimes we just need a brief conversation with a like-minded Christian and a moment of prayer. Then, taking a deep breath, forge on.

The Bible says that a merry heart is as good as medicine, but a broken spirit dries the bones (Proverbs 17:22). Frequently, our perspective needs a paradigm shift. We cannot constantly be upset, hurt and worried. I know it can be hard but work on being happy. Talk to a good friend or a therapist. If you cannot wrap your head around happy, at least praise God for his presence in your life. Even if you do not feel Him, He is there.

Chapter 3
STEPS OF FAITH VS. DARTS OF DOUBTS

Our decision to keep Jordan at home was an enormous step of faith, but we did not realize it at the time. The responsibility of his daily care became very intense, but in our simple belief that God would provide, He did. Some of His provision included financial resources, a loving caregiver, friends, faith, and patience.

Without God and His provision, we would have likely needed to place Jordan outside our home. If for some reason we determined that it would be best for our family not to have Jordan present due to an adverse change in his behavior, or should his health issues become more than we could deal with, we would need to reconsider. Paul and I also realized that we would not live forever, so eventually changes in Jordan's residence would need to be made. Even with the knowledge that keeping Jordan at home was right for us, living out that decision — not easy. Statistics told me that the repercussions could potentially destroy my family. I determined within myself that it would not. Again, I turned to the Bible.

I was reminded life is what we make it. Feeling

sorry for myself did not help or change anything for the better, but it could certainly make things worse. For example: Proverbs 18:21 says that *life and death are in the power of the tongue.* I worked on speaking only good, positive, and faith-filled words, even when I didn't think or feel it. When I told you about the time Jordan's seizure broke his permanent front teeth, I cried. My friend reminded me, it could have been his head. In the moment, I did not think good thoughts, but fortunately, I did not speak bad thoughts. Speak what you want.

• *God, I believe you have paved the way for Jordan's future.*

Philippians 4:4 says, *Rejoice in the Lord always. Again I say, rejoice!* I think the apostle Paul repeated himself because he knew it would not be easy to rejoice, for example, when my child, so gravely ill, needed to be hospitalized. Some things we need to hear over and over again. I am rejoicing, God. Rejoice by faith, even when you don't feel it. We need to remind ourselves that we have a Comforter named Holy Spirit (John 14:26), part of the Godhead: the Father, the Son and the Holy Spirit. Don't try to do everything on your own. Take a deep breath and pray. Start thanking God for His comfort as you walk the path you are on, rejoice that you are not alone. He is always with you, even when you may not feel Him.

• *God, I need the Holy Spirit, my Comforter.*

Philippians 4:6-7 says not to be worried about anything. Really God? Yes! For every need, petition God earnestly, prayerfully, humbly and with confidence that what you need has already been accomplished. The peace of God that actually surpasses your understanding will guard your heart and mind. Those verses told me that if I began to worry, I should pray to keep my heart soft toward God and life, so I would not lose my sanity. I would not focus on my fears, what I did not want. When you focus on the positive, you are more courageous, positive and strong. It gives you energy. When you dwell on the bad, the what if's, the fears, you feel depressed, weak, and tired. Over time worry makes one sick: high blood pressure, ulcers, heart problems, depression, even obesity can come from worry. So much of what is mental becomes physical. Keep your mind focused on Christ. With every bad thought say, *Thank-you God for victory!* Again, say what you are believing for, not what you see or what you fear. Say what you want.

• *God, thank You for courage.*

Philippians 4:13 says, *I can do all things through Christ who strengthens me*. That told me that I could and would get through as I depended on God for my strength. I knew my own strength was not enough. I can do this; I will do this. It became a theme for me. I passed this truth to my children. I remember talking to my daughter, Morgan, about fears she experienced thinking about her parts in a play, a speech, a test. Be patient and calm: "Morgan, you can do this; even when you feel you can't, you can. Even when you don't want to, you will." No back door. You can do this when you set your mind.

• *God, I will get through this. Thank You for your strength.*

Philippians 4:19 says, *And my God shall supply all your need according to his riches in glory by Christ Jesus*. The realities of Jordan's continuing needs went beyond anything I could have imagined or even feared; way, way beyond my natural ability to cope. Confronted with a myriad of situations constantly, Jordan's expenses were sometimes out of control; there were appointments on top of appointments. There were times I knew Jordan's issues better than a doctor. His health became extremely complex, and very unusual. Sometimes, the medical field personnel did not listen. For the most part, I weeded through the uncooperative, egotistical, arrogant health-care providers, and was primarily rewarded with the best. For that, I thank God for his provision. When we needed to replace our caregiver, we found someone uniquely qualified. God is not our personal magician, but He is moved by faith. God always answers prayer. For reasons I do not fully understand, and frankly do not appreciate, sometimes God's answer is no. Jordan did not receive his healing during his earthly lifetime, and yet, I saw God do amazing things in His provision for our family.

- *God, I need a caregiver for Jordan.*
- *God, I need favor with this person who is telling me no.*
- *God, I need You!*

There are so many additional scriptures that became alive and real to me in a different way. The scriptures have always been truth, and they have always been available to me as a Christian. However, if you don't study to know the character and promises of God through His Word, it is hard to avail yourself of the benefits.

I experienced many moments of frustration, sadness, and even anger, but when I stopped and turned to God's Word, the Comforter, who is the Holy Spirit, I was reminded, *Debbie, you are not alone.* God continues to be with us, and I have peace (John 14:26 – 27).

DARTS OF DOUBT

Even for people of faith, the devil is a force to be reckoned with. I know what I believe and I know the devil is defeated. I also recognize that the devil is not going to leave me alone simply because I want him to or because I am a Christian. In fact, as Christians, we are a target for the devil. He likes to try to mess with our thinking. The devil is waiting, hovering, poised — like a cat waiting to pounce on a mouse — for an opportunity. John 10:10a says, *The devil does not come except to steal, and to kill, and to destroy.*

Satan throws darts of doubt at us in the form of thoughts or maybe vague impressions. I don't think anyone is immune to having darts of doubt enter our consciousness. If we grab onto one of those thoughts and begin to meditate, we will begin to fear or doubt, but if we refuse to grab onto these thoughts, they cannot take root and will just pass through. Fear and doubt are the devil's greatest tools, but we have authority to take control when we understand God's Word. The Bible says in Hosea 4:6, *My people are destroyed for lack of knowledge...*

Reading and understanding God's Word means we can also know God's character. That knowledge brings strength and confidence. My husband and I have needed every bit of it. Believing in God, and understanding God's Word are two different things. You can believe in God and go to Heaven when you die without understanding the many truths, and without experiencing the benefits of God's Word during your lifetime.

For reasons I do not fully understand, when we pray, we do not always get what we want when we want it. I hate that! Our prayers are always answered, but sometimes God says no. I do not know why God did not heal Jordan's body, why he died, and I won't know until I get to Heaven. When I arrive at Heaven's gates, I believe all will be revealed. At that time, it will make sense to me. In the meantime, I walk by faith.

In Matthew 7:24-27, Jesus is talking about two men who both believed in God. He said, whoever hears and obeys Him is like a wise man who built his house on a rock; when the rain came with terrible floods and wind beating against the house it would stand, being solidly built. Those who did not listen and obey, like those who built their homes on sand, were unstable. When the floods, rains, and winds came, the house fell. One man understood and believed what God taught, thus able to withstand the challenges in life. The other man, although a believer, remained foolish and did not understand, and did not follow God's Word. Being weak he could not weather the storms of life. His life fell apart, the marriage failed, the family came apart, and pain and confusion reigned.

From the day God spoke it, the truth of His Word has not changed. The Bible says: *Take up the whole armor of God that you may be able to withstand in the evil day, and having done all, to stand* (Ephesians 6:13). Get equipped with the Word of God; it is your armor, and we need armor to do battle. When you make the truths from the Word of God part of your life, it gives you confidence. You don't feel powerless in the face of challenging circumstances. Don't give in.

Therefore do not cast away your confidence, which has great reward (Hebrews 10:35). You must have confidence in the Word of God. Trust Him to make a way. Keep walking by faith. Say what you want is yours, stubbornly; do not stop believing. Regardless of circumstances, regardless of what you don't see, stand your ground. Don't give up.

James 5:16b says, *The effectual, fervent prayer of a righteous man*/mom (The Willis Translation) *avails much.* Fervent means passionate, enthusiastic, and fanatical — as in, *Get-out-of-my-way, mother coming through!* Righteous means moral, good, just, and forgiven. The Bible says to pray continually, without ceasing. That does not mean you are mumbling constantly. It means to have an attitude of prayer. Talk to God. That's what prayer is, just talking to God. A decision needs to be made? Ask God what He thinks. If you are walking into an appointment, say, "Okay, here we go, Father. Thank you for giving me wisdom." God is not going to make decisions for you, but you may feel the unction of the Holy Spirit, a knowing of what to do. **Don't stop praying.**

Get yourself prepared spiritually before the next hard place in your life arrives. Nobody slides through life without challenges. Bad things happen to all people. The Word says that the just would live by faith, but how do you build your faith if you never need to use it? While it is never a big thrill to encounter hard situations, when you know that our Lord and Savior is there to guide, guard, and govern, it is not so scary.

I told a friend of mine going through her personal challenge with cancer that I knew my life experience gave me a really nifty testimony, but frankly, I would rather have spent time in a spa. Faith challenges are not fun to go through, but the important thing is you can go through it without losing your faith. God never leaves us on our own.

Paul and I attended church for many years prior to Jordan's birth. We took the opportunity to study the Bible. We knew God, His character, His love, His plan for us as believers. We attended intimate Bible studies where we discussed our challenges, fears, and behavior, both good and bad. We took out all our baggage from the past and sorted through it, resolving what we could and accepting what we could not. We cleaned our mental houses as best we could and began to renew our minds to God's Word (Romans 12:1-2).

If you are a new Christian and think you are not yet spiritually prepared, don't feel that you have lost out. While I believe the more you exercise your faith muscle, the stronger it becomes, you can still successfully walk through a dark place in your life. In the process, you will learn much during your journey.

There are some scriptures in Mark that show how God will help us even when we feel weak. A man asked Jesus for his son's healing, and in Mark 9:23-24 it says, *Jesus said to him, If you can believe, all things are possible to him who believes. Immediately the father of the child cried out and said with tears, Lord, I believe; help my unbelief!* That father must have touched God's heart.

Even today, after many years as a Christian, I have said, "Lord, help my unbelief," as well. One never arrives when it comes to faith. We get stronger as we experience life, but we never stop exercising our faith. The Bible says in Romans 12:2, *And do not be conformed to this world, but be transformed by the renewing of your mind, that ye may prove what is that good and acceptable and perfect will of God.* Living by faith is a process of growth and renewal to God's Word. That growth process never ends.

You may wonder if you can truly live by faith. I am here to tell you that yes, you can. Start by getting a Bible you can understand. Some people have purchased a child's Bible, others have first read a youth Bible. Some start with, The Message, also a Bible, that reads more like a book. As you are reading, start praying every day. Devoting specific time to both read and pray daily is a really good thing, but also have an attitude of prayer. Talk to God frequently, make Him your friend. More than anything, God wants a relationship with you. Yes, it is possible. He already loves you. Regardless of your past, good or bad, God loves you right now.

Chapter 4
FRIENDS ARE IMPORTANT

In addition to having knowledge and understanding of God's Word, and believing the truth of it, having strong relationships is vital. These relationships may not necessarily be your *family*, those to whom you are related by blood or marriage. For a variety of reasons, for the most part, neither of our families were available to be of practical help. Illnesses, distance, jobs and personal issues kept our families away. We asked for help on occasion, but it was not usually readily or freely forthcoming. My mother, Clineene Smith, came when the kids were born, but she lived some distance from me, was not always well, and did not drive. She is a strong Christian and prayed for our family fervently. Paul's mother, Lillian Willis, bless her heart, was a wonderful grandmother and gave every spare moment to help us in any way she possibly could. Being involved in her own battle with cancer, while her desire to help was very evident, she was not able. She died when Jordan was four. I am very sad she did not survive to enjoy our children, and they with her. One of my sisters lived out of state for many years, and the other also lived quite a distance away, which was not practical. We chose not to broadcast Jordan's challenges openly to every family member, so some were not given the opportunity to help, even if they wanted to. We did not want to have to deal with unbelief from those who could not operate in faith. We did not have the energy to address their questions and concerns. The relationships you need are with like-minded people who are close by and can provide encouragement, prayer, faith, and sometimes, practical assistance on your behalf. My husband and I found most of these relationships with people in our church, Christian Faith Center, located in Federal Way, Washington, a suburb of Seattle.

EXAMPLES OF FRIENDSHIP

Jordan was a social person and he liked to touch people. Sometimes his touching was harder than an actual touch, more like a smack. One day in the mall, he wandered away quickly when I let go of his hand for a moment. He walked up to a strange woman and gave her one of his generous heart-felt whacks. She perceived this as him hitting her, and she hit him back. Upset that he got away from us, I became embarrassed that Jordan exhibited such antisocial behavior. He didn't think he did anything wrong and couldn't understand all the drama. The woman he *touched* realized that she hit a disabled person, and she, too, was embarrassed.

While trying to straighten all this out, nobody watched Jordan – again! He was merrily running amok down the mall, happy as a lark. I was absolutely horrified that in such a short time span the same thing happened; we lost track of him twice in one day. I felt like a negligent, irresponsible, bad mother. It sickened me, and I took it very hard; another reminder of how disabled Jordan was. When I told my friend and co-worker about it, she laughed. It made me feel better, and I could see the humor, like something from a comedy show.

Sometimes, we have needed practical help. Around Jordan's third birthday, Paul and I planned a business trip to San Francisco. I think it may have been our first trip away since Jordan was born, and Heaven knows we needed the break. We arranged for care for Jordan, a trusted friend, who was experienced with him. Two days before we left, Jordan came down with chickenpox. Our friend was not able to care for him, and under those circumstances I couldn't leave town. I did not think I wanted to go anyway with my baby sick. Another friend, very familiar with Jordan, because she was his daycare teacher at church, volunteered to move into our house with her husband and two children. Her children just recovered from chickenpox. Our friend knew we needed to get a break. To me, her sacrifice seemed so great, and I accepted her offer with gratitude. I felt comfortable enough with her experience to leave him. It is wonderful the way God blessed us through our many relationships.

Our church family volunteered to perform physical therapy on Jordan for more than a year to help him learn to walk. The therapy involved dozens of people on a rotating basis — five people, three times a day, five days a week — who came to our church daycare for Jordan's daily exercises. The task of finding people to help with these exercises was completely overwhelming to me. My friend, Darlene Anderson, came to my office one day and found me very distressed. I told her of our need. She said not to think another thing about it, she would take care of it. I can feel the relief decades later, and it still brings tears to my eyes.

Think about this: my boss allowed his staff members to stop whatever was going on with their own responsibilities, at designated times during the day, five days a week for well over a year. Our staff and other volunteers came, with fantastic attitudes, and exercised Jordan faithfully. What a gift. I will talk more about Jordan's therapy and treatments later.

On one Thanksgiving Day, preparing dinner for what would be a houseful of guests, Jordan fell during a seizure and broke his front tooth. Yes, the teeth again. His dentist, Dr. Patrick Fleege, gave us his home telephone number long before because, in spite of a protective helmet, we had already experienced so many tooth emergencies. The phone number in itself was an incredible kindness. Paul called the dentist and the dentist's wife, also a dentist, answered. She said her husband went duck hunting, but she would try to reach him and give him the information. Within 20 minutes, we received a callback. We were instructed to bring Jordan into the office. Paul took him. Both the dentists worked together and repaired the damaged tooth as I continued cooking dinner at home. Paul and Jordan were home before our family and guests arrived. Thanksgiving and life went on. We would not allow these incidents to have much impact on our lives; it was one way to have victory over the devil.

Even with the Holy Spirit to comfort us, we need the practical help and strength that faith-filled people provide. During Jordan's brain surgery, our friend, Randy Lagerquist, came to sit with Paul and me. She just sat quietly with us in the hospital room for many hours. She provided a calm strength to help us keep our own. During his hospital recovery, a couple of our friends came to spend the night with him, one of them a neurological nurse. We went home and slept like logs.

PEOPLE WANT TO HELP

When someone dies, or an emergency happens, one of the things friends will ask is if there is anything they can do to help. They are sincere. They want to help. Unfortunately, at that moment, you haven't a clue of what you need. The offer is made, but you don't have a response, so the offer might wither and die on the vine. What is extra nice is when someone just finds a need and fills it.

I am usually on the giving side, but sometimes if I needed something I often did not think to ask for help. Maybe I did not even recognize a need, but when someone else saw a way to help and took it upon themselves to do it, it was a huge blessing. I would often weep with relief. People truly want to help.

I am gifted in some areas and have no patience for other areas. When my children graduated from high school, I found some activities were traditions that needed my involvement. I am not always fond of tradition. For example, every graduate received an assigned table in which to display their awards, examples of their interests, special photos of their family or experiences, as well as the all-important decorated box for cards. I may have enjoyed putting that together at one time in my life, but it seemed like an irritating task during those high school years. My assistant and friend, Annie Carr-Elder, absolutely loves helping people and is creative. She just took over that project, on her own time, and created wonderful tables for my children. She was so excited about it, you would have concluded I did her a favor, instead of the other way around. When I gave parties, Annie would serve in my kitchen, making sure everything went well. What a gift.

Another assistant and friend, Debra Popejoy, earned one of her university degrees in hospitality. As the media director at our church, I held strategy meetings every quarter. We brought in experts from out-of-town, deciding television programming, what product we needed to develop, and fundraising ideas to support the media ministry during the next quarter. Debra put together refreshments and lunch. She made it so easy for me. At one time, I really enjoyed entertaining, but in my current circumstances, I felt it stressful rather than fun. Debra, however, loved it. When she or I decided it might be nice to have a dinner party at my home, she would help me plan. We would go out and buy supplies for fabulous invitations, come up with a theme and a menu. Debra's husband just happened to be a chef and did catering. Very fun for both of us, being able to entertain the way I did before all the complications. It made me happy.

I am most definitely not a shopper. If I need a pair of black pants, I go to the store (or go online now), and buy the pants; get-in and get-out. Well, I have a daughter who loves to shop (groan);

I mean loves it! One year before school started she really wanted to go shopping. I wanted her to have fun, but I quite simply did not have it in me to make it a fun day for her. I have a friend, Theresa Fazekas, the CFO of Christian Faith Center and an extraordinarily busy woman, who is a shopping queen. I sort of apologetically asked her if she would mind taking Morgan school shopping. Her eyes lit up; a smile spread across her face and she said she would love to! Morgan and Aunt Theresa experienced a wonderful, long shopping day. The next school year they did it again. Morgan is a grown woman now, and they are still shopping buddies. I have learned that sometimes they text during a church service about a particular dress they saw someone wearing, or a sale at the mall. Morgan sometimes helps Theresa in her home as a server for parties. They have the best relationship that likely would not have happened if I never asked for Theresa's help. God's people have made a huge difference in our lives.

We walked in grace every day. Friends, neighbors, and family were always supportive, and some extraordinarily helpful. Every step of the way, God provided who and what we needed, when we needed it. Self-reliance is great, but sometimes your needs are beyond you! Ask for what you need! If one person cannot help, another will.

HOW TO BEGIN FRIENDSHIPS

Friendships are an area of strength for me. I have learned to talk to anybody. My family says I can talk to a wall, and it will respond. My husband is more reserved and takes the scenic route to friendship. I just start talking. If you find you have little to nothing in common, or if the person is not going down a path you want to follow, the budding friendship will likely drop off your radar. Whatever your route, when you begin to build friendships, do so with people who are like-minded, strong in areas in which you might want to be stronger. Friendship is a give and take relationship, each imparting to the other. There are different levels of friendship, casual to intimate. I am not talking sexual, but where you can talk to each other about anything, having each other's trust. For some, you can pick up a conversation right where you left off, even years later.

A great place to start finding friends is to attend and volunteer at church or a non-profit. The possibility of finding a like-minded friend is pretty strong if you have a specific interest in common. If there are activities planned for your age group at an event, go. If you put forth effort, you will make friends. You need friends and friends need you. Just start talking.

Chapter 5
MARRIAGE

This chapter is a little long. I considered editing it down, but there is so much to say about marriage that I could not! Statistics show many, many families with constant high levels of stress are dysfunctional, or they just plain fall apart. My marriage and family are very functional, strong, and happy. Before hard times hit, you need to know what your marriage is made of — convenience or commitment. Convenience is for as long as it feels good. Commitment is for as long as I live, till death do us part. No back doors. We are very appreciative of each other, and we do not take for granted the benefits we have. We recognize that our blessings are gifts from God. Our marriage relationship has been tested and tried. We have overcome and succeeded, not based on love alone, but also on our commitment to each other, our children, God, and our friends and family.

Married for 15 years before Jordan arrived, I honestly did not plan to ever have children. At the time I became pregnant, a permanent solution to birth control was a topic of discussion. Too late! When I learned I was having a baby, to say I was shocked is the least of it; a more apt description would be horrified. When I talked to Paul about the pregnancy, he smiled and was actually pretty tickled about it. Frankly, that made me kind of irritated. I went on a little tirade and told him that we are partners in this, and that each would share half the work. I was awful. He still smiled and said he would do that, and he did. For example, when Jordan needed to be fed, Paul got up in the middle of the night, changed his diaper and brought him to me. I fed him, and Paul put him back to bed. He has been an amazing husband and father.

I don't know how my bad thinking about children started. I never liked babysitting. I never allowed our guests to bring their children to our home while entertaining. My sister-in-law lectured her children before going to Aunt Debbie's house, that they needed to be extra special good.

GUILT AND STRESS

I really worked on my attitude during my pregnancy. I prayed, and I studied. I went shopping for maternity clothes. I went shopping for baby clothes. I decorated the nursery. I really, really tried to get into it, and the best I can say is, by the time of his birth, I wanted to want Jordan because I knew I was so wrong. Then to give birth to a child with special needs felt like punishment for my bad attitude about children. Regardless of my anger, I knew in my heart of hearts that this was not a punishment from God, but I still felt guilty and responsible.

Jordan's birth came with illness and disabilities. Plagued with guilt, I took the fault and blamed myself because before birth I did not love or want him. I hadn't prayed for him during my entire pregnancy. At birth, when I saw and heard him, I totally fell in love with him. It did not, however, ease my guilt. I found a scripture that ultimately helped. The Bible says, *And above all things have fervent love for one another, for "love will cover a multitude of sins,"* (I Peter 4:8). I totally loved that baby beyond anything I had ever experienced. My husband never blamed me for Jordan's inabilities. It took some time, but I finally forgave myself.

WILL HE STAY OR WILL HE GO?

I come from a family of divorce, with a great deal of dreadful thinking in me about marriage and trust. I carried a lot of hurts. Raised in church, I knew God loved me, although I cannot say I felt close to Him. I did, however, have a foundational understanding of God's Word. Way before children, I became involved with the Washington Drug Rehabilitation Center (WDRC) a program founded on Christian principles, and the program in which our pastor, Casey Treat, became rehabilitated from drug addiction. During this time, I recommitted my life to God. It did not *fix* me, and I still carried with me a lot of pain from my past. My initial involvement with WDRC started with attending a community group program. I did not have a drug or alcohol problem, but I did have a marriage in trouble. Paul and I seemed on the brink of separating. Someone I encountered suggested I might find help there. A drug rehabilitation community group? My first reaction — you gotta be kidding?! In the past, I tried therapy and marriage counseling; I finally decided, what could it hurt?

WDRC was founded by a most unlikely man, a former convict named Julius Young. His testimony was a true miracle. Julius now resides in Heaven. He spent the majority of his life in a high-security prison, a truly bad and evil man. Somehow, God got ahold of him. Julius made a jailhouse promise to God; if there could ever be a way to be released from prison, he would spend the remainder of his life helping people. Ultimately, Julius, serving a sentence that should have lasted for decades, probably life, was released, and he later founded WDRC. As I wrote earlier, one of the program clients, Casey Treat, became a resident in the program — to avoid jail time — got clean, was saved, went to Bible college, and founded Christian Faith Center with his wife, Wendy. They have helped hundreds of thousands of people, likely more, including Paul and myself. I have tried to find Julius' prison record but have concluded he may have changed his name upon release. I hope those who had been closest to him will someday write a biography about his life.

When I started attending a WDRC community outreach group, Paul saw changes in me and eventually joined me. We began to work on our relationship. Part of that work became recognizing our very wrong thinking about ourselves and each other, and replacing the old thinking for new, godly thoughts. Romans 12:1-2 says, *I beseech you therefore, brethren, by the mercies of God, that you present your bodies a living sacrifice, holy, acceptable to God, which is your reasonable service. And do not be conformed to this world, but be transformed by the renewing of your mind, that you may prove what is that good and acceptable and perfect will of God.* Renewing the mind is replacing your bad thinking for God's good thoughts. It is as simple and as hard as that!

Paul comes from a family of illness. He was about five when his father, Don Willis, fell out of a tree while building a vacation cabin. Doctors told Paul's mother her husband would not survive. Then she was told he would live, but never walk again. Paul's dad did live, and he did walk again, but his health from that time on became very fragile. He was often close to death's door. Paul's issue with illness was huge; in fact, he pretty much hated it. My mother pampered me during illness. This became a problem: our opposite thinking about illness. When Paul joined me by attending WDRC community groups, our marriage relationship vastly improved. Paul attended church on occasion as a boy, but he became born again in 1980 at the founding of Christian Faith Center. Paul's issue with illness, however, remained.

Before we took Jordan home from the hospital, we met a couple of times with a social worker who tried to prepare us for the reality of what the future held in the years to come from her perspective. Even though her advice came from an ungodly perspective, her information proves sadly true for many people in our situation. According to statistics, fathers do not do well, in the long term, with the stress, inconvenience, the money and time commitment of dealing with a chronically ill, mentally or physically disabled child. They very often abandon their families. Jordan met all of those conditions. Maybe Paul *chewed* on the information from those hospital meetings, or maybe he just felt the need to reassure me, but sometime later he sincerely told me that he would not be one of those men. He would not leave us; in it for the long haul, whatever that would come to mean. Until he said that, I did not know how much I needed to hear it. Our bond became stronger.

In addition to all the challenges of normal married life, including a demanding business, my work, a large home, our other children, and volunteering, the stress of Jordan sometimes put us over the top. We loved him, but his needs — were extreme.

THE STRAIN STARTED SHOWING

I began to be subject to panic attacks. The first one was extraordinarily frightening. My day began with Jordan falling out of the back of Paul's pick-up. The gate of the truck bed went up to Jordan's chest. We both believed him to be safe. In an instant, he was having a full blown, grand mal seizure, descending head first out of the truck. He smashed to the ground where he landed on his forehead. We could immediately see the start of a huge egg-sized bump.

Heading to a doctor did not occur to us, but maybe I should have gone for myself! I remember the balance of the day was extraordinarily busy. My blood pressure was likely soaring. At the end of the day, leaving to go home, I was more than ready. Just before leaving to get Mr. J-man, a request came from my boss's wife asking me to stop by a frame shop on my way home to pick out a molding for a custom frame. Really? I just wanted to get out of there.

That request must have pushed my body and brain over the top. After I picked up Jordan, whose goose egg turned a terrible black and blue, I put him in his car seat and began the drive to the frame shop. Without warning, my world began to fade, going from gray to black, as I passed out! *Oh, Jesus, help, help!* I managed to get to the side of the road, and I completely blacked out. When I came around, the car still running in drive, my foot on the brake, Jordan sleeping with his banged up head, I assume I was only out for a few seconds. Recovered, I went about my business. God forbid I would use a little common sense and get help. No, no way. I just forged on! What a dope!

The next time it happened, the sun simply moved behind a cloud; it must have triggered the feeling of fading away similar to when I passed out before. I began to hyperventilate. This time, I recognized the situation. I turned up the air-conditioning and the radio to full blast, rolled down the windows and started singing at the top of my lungs — anything to distract myself. I needed to normalize my breathing, which would stop the feeling of panic. For years after that whenever the sun went behind a cloud, I felt the start of panic: I started to hyperventilate, sweat, and shake. I would always pray and then sing at the top of my lungs. Sometimes, I would plan something pleasant in my head. My parents' anniversary was coming up, plan a party... eventually the attacks stopped.

Blake was about a year old when Paul arrived home to find Jordan and Blake locked in their bedrooms, and me locked in our bathroom. I heard him call for me, and I tried to get myself together, but I couldn't — not happening. He found me and discovered the door locked. Through the door, he asked if everything was okay, and I said, "No." He asked me to unlock the door, and I replied, "No." Then he said, "Honey, you need to open the door." Totally embarrassed that he found me in such a mess, I finally opened the door, my head hanging low. He starting to question me, I told him:

I don't think I can do this any more.

What can't you do any more?

All of this, Jordan, Blake, the house, my job. This is beyond me, I can't do it.

Okay, you don't have to. We will get some help.

I think I appeared so capable he was not aware of my needs, and I had not communicated what those needs were. Honestly, what a martyr! Too much pride, I guess. Maybe I thought of my, *I can do it all attitude* as a dictum of faith.We had previously hired a little help for house cleaning, but from that time on, we employed a nanny for the kids. You may be thinking, *well, that's all well and good for you, but I cannot afford that!* Hold on, because I have a few ideas later on that might help start some creative brainstorming. We can become derailed too easily in our endeavors when we cannot immediately find a solution.

RHONDA

For several years, a wonderful nanny and housekeeper, Mary Anderson, took care of our home, but our Mary Poppins came in the person of Rhonda Berg. I don't know how I would have survived without Rhonda. She came to work for us when Jordan was 8, Blake 5 and Morgan 2. Rhonda's experience as an aide in a special education classroom prepared her, but her younger brother, Kevin, who is a genius with computers, was born with cerebral palsy, which made her uniquely qualified; young and enthusiastic with a very positive attitude. We loved her, but more important, she loved our children, especially Jordan. In addition to all her qualifications, Rhonda was also a committed Christian. When you hire someone as an employee, there are certain questions that are illegal to ask, but I needed to know if she loved the Lord. During our interview I asked her if my children got hurt or not feeling well would she be willing to pray with them for healing. Her face lit up, and she said, "Absolutely!"

Eventually, Rhonda married. Her husband, Greg Jones, recognized early in their courtship that Rhonda and Jordan came as a package deal. He wanted them both. God provided for us in an amazing way. Eventually, Rhonda and I realized that Blake and Morgan no longer needed a nanny. Rhonda asked if she could take Jordan to live with her. When that happened, we continued to talk to each other almost daily, sometimes several times a day. We worked out a schedule that allowed her time off and kept us intimately in the loop of Jordan's care. This worked well, with a bedroom in both of our homes, clothing, his own televisions, two sets of books, videos, and puzzles; in essence, two homes with two mothers and two fathers.

With Rhonda and Greg, Jordan experienced things he might not have otherwise. They loved boating and swimming and camping. They took Jordan along with them and exposed him to many great experiences. Rhonda would call and say, we need a trailer to hook onto the back of Greg's bike. We are taking Jordan with us bike riding. Jordan needs a life-jacket...Jordan needs an umbrella for the beach...Jordan needs water slippers, we're going to the water park...Jordan needs money for a movie and popcorn...Jordan is going camping with us. That kid was so well loved. Rhonda and Greg's care of Jordan gave Paul and me some relief, reduced the stress load, and helped us keep our marriage and family strong. God blessed us at the right time.

You might be wondering how we could afford all of this. Frankly, the answer would take another whole book. I will simply quote William Cowper (1731-1800) who wrote, "God moves in a mysterious way, His wonders to perform." We have always been obedient and faithful in tithing (Malachi 3), and God promises that when we are faithful over little, He will make us rulers over much. God knew what we would need way before we did. He is Jehovah Jireh, our Provider; full of love and grace. We are not financially rich, but we are financially prosperous. You can share in God's prosperity, too. Get into His Word, and read or listen to financial books written by smart, Christian authors. You probably will not experience overnight financial success, but you can develop that area of your life. Money makes life easier, but it does not make you happy. Some Christians think that money is evil, but the Bible does not say that. The Bible says that the love of money is the root of evil. I don't love money, but I use it for what I want and what I need.

STRATEGY FOR FUNDS

It is critical to carve out some alone time, either really alone with yourself or with your spouse or friends; time to laugh, take a walk, talk, go out to dinner. Mental rest is refreshing, but often it comes with a need for money for childcare. This will not be an exhaustive study, but I want to give you a few ideas to open up your creative thinking regarding fundraising to meet your needs for rest and relaxation. You may not like these, but perhaps they will launch you into finding a way. I once did some financial counseling and these ideas are from that time.

First and foremost, the absolute easiest way to obtain funds is to stop purchasing coffee beverages. In helping a woman once to balance her budget, she was about $200 short in her finances every month. I found most of it in her coffee purchases. She called it her small daily reward. That amount of money could buy you a date or two. The lady bought a bag of coffee, some flavored creamer and made her own. Voila! Extra money!

Other easy ideas are: turn off lights when you leave a room, turn down heat and wear a sweater, time your showers to three minutes, clip coupons. Honestly, these add up.

Another easy way to raise funds is to barter services. What do you have to offer in exchange for childcare? Are you a hairdresser, manicurist, massage therapist, gardener, seamstress, cook? Are you a whiz at balancing checkbooks or writing checks to pay bills, like a bookkeeper? Do you like to iron?

Do you have a spare room in your home that you could offer for rent or in exchange for childcare; maybe a combination for both? Could a child share a room with a sibling to free up space? You could give up your own room if there is an en-suite; that would bring in several hundred dollars. I understand it is not a fun idea, but it would work for extra funds.

Our young friend, Monica Croonquist (nee Anderson), whose parents served as missionaries in the Philippines, lived with us off and on for several years. Her rent consisted of performing physical therapy exercises on Jordan and some babysitting. It was fabulous! She was superb with the Jordan-boy. We love her still.

I am sure, as you meditate, you will come up with more ideas. It is well worth the effort.

THE WORKING MOTHER DILEMMA

I could have quit my job and stopped volunteering to stay home and meet the needs of my family, but Paul knew I needed an outlet. I worked because I loved it. The money that I earned went to support our household help and Jordan's expenses, which allowed me to continue to work. At one point my income pushed us into a higher income-tax bracket, and we actually lost money because I worked.

I worked because I wanted to! It gave me space to breath, and not think about the challenges at home. Income aside, I enjoyed using my gifts and talents. I found with Jordan's incredible needs, I could no longer work full-time. My boss allowed me to take the responsibilities I enjoyed to carve out a part-time job. What a gift! I was very capable and found I could handle a great deal of responsibility in short periods. Flexible with receiving phone calls during my off-hours, and sometimes working additional hours; it all worked beautifully.

Having a child, even a special needs child, does not need to be the end of a mother's career. I believe women should give themselves permission to work—full-time, part-time, or not at all. It is a choice. If circumstances had forced me to stay home...well, it would not have been a pretty picture. I worked part-time the majority of my career.

FIGHT RIGHT AND DATE

My husband is an extremely patient man. We went for many months without sex. I think it may have been after Jordan's brain surgery. So far beyond my ability to cope with all the needs, I shut down in that area. I tried, but Paul knew it was simply to please him. That was not the kind of sex he wanted. He just said when I was ready to let him know. It took a long time, poor guy. With his loving kindness toward me, my love for him grew. Marriage is a long-term commitment. When you think of it that way, you will do everything you can to make it good. Challenges along the way are just that — challenges. Some challenges take longer than others to resolve. When both husband and wife are committed to the marriage relationship, and in good faith do all they can do — including seeking counseling when necessary — the relationship will survive and thrive even in the greatest challenges.

After being married for two or three decades, someone asked us our secret to a long-term marriage. My husband responded with, "No back door." Make the decision when you get married, there is *one* way in and no way out. With that concept, you will work hard at working on your relationship — you have to fight for your marriage. It takes effort. You do not want to be bound in a miserable relationship. It takes determination to build a happy family.

One of the scriptures I think of is Ephesians 6:13 (KJV): *and therefore take up the whole armor of God that you may be able to withstand in the evil day, and having* **done all,** *to* **stand.** Stand for your marriage. The marriage relationship, in general, can sometimes be difficult; a marriage with built-in, high-stress situations needs extra care, understanding, and prayer. It also needs fun.

For many, many years, Paul and I scheduled a date night. If you think this is outside your budget, go back a few pages to fundraising, and read it again. We found a very qualified caregiver and went out once a week; usually, a dinner and a movie. Sometimes, we left from the front door, went around the house to our sliding bedroom doors, and spent a very quiet evening at home. Couples need time together; time to talk, time to hold hands and kiss, time to communicate in privacy. Before becoming parents, you were a couple. Your marriage will still be there when your kids leave home. You don't want to be married to a stranger. You also need time to fight.

Couples need to take time to clear the air. As a little girl, I hated hearing my parents argue. Ultimately ineffective, they ended up in divorce. Paul and I are committed to each other. We know we will never divorce, but we also know we need to communicate our differences, and sometimes that includes arguing. When the kids were small, we waited until they went to bed and then we went as far away as possible from their bedrooms, and we talked. Arguing does not necessarily mean shouting, and Paul and I rarely — like, less than the count on a single hand — actually shout at each other. As the children got older, we would go up to our bedroom and close the door to talk it out. They knew that a closed door meant knock, and wait for a response, before entering.

If it becomes very late, with the argument going nowhere, and it is evident that a resolution will not be forthcoming, we agree to disagree. We agree to start the process again at a better time. We will work out the problem or disagreement, but just not right then. That kind of arguing takes mutual respect, maturity, commitment, and determination. Yes, you can still be angry, and yes, you still need to work it out, but remember it is not a contest, it is not a race. A little distance or time can make the solution clearer. Sometimes arguing is more about pride than being right or wrong.

I know about the scripture of not allowing the sun to go down on your wrath (Ephesians 4:26

KJV), but really droning on, even when you are running in circles in your anger and fatigue, is really not smart. You will not get very far in achieving resolution and closure that way. If you can be mature and agree to delay the continuation of the argument, put aside your bad attitude, bad temper, pride or whatever and be the husband/wife that would be pleasing to God, then do it. Simply agree to disagree, and take a break.

During an argument, never, never, ever walk out the door in a huff. It makes for high drama when the door slams, but it plants the seed of distrust, even divorce. Say you need a break, and with your spouse's agreement, do something else for awhile; go pray somewhere, go for a run, go for a drive, exercise, or do mindless laundry – whatever – then come back together at a specified time. Always argue in good faith, with the goal being to work things out, not to be right.

If you have not been smart to argue in private, and your children have heard you, they will be upset, regardless of their age. Reassure them that all is well, and you love each other and them. Their security, especially when they are young with built-in stressors like a Jordan, is vital. Insecure kids will act out in a multitude of negative ways.

KEEP YOUR PRIORITIES RIGHT IN MARRIAGE

In addition to working, I also volunteered. Sometimes when you work for a church, the line between working and volunteering becomes blurred. Sometimes a staff member consistently volunteers to work so many unpaid overtime hours that it becomes the equivalent of an additional employee — without the benefit of added income. Over the long term, it is not fair. There are many expectations from not only the senior pastors but also the congregation. The pastors are growing their church, similar to a business owner building his or her business. They are passionate about everything. Their vision is to meet the needs of as many people as possible.

The congregation often expects the staff to be at every event. If enough of the staff does not populate a certain event, some church members get upset. They figure if they take the time to volunteer, the staff ought to be there, too. In reality, there is something going on almost every day and night at church that is important to someone. It is impossible to do it all, but the expectations are pretty high.

I began to realize that no matter how much I did it would never be enough. I needed to prioritize my life to meet all the needs. I began to say "No" to some things, and that did not make me popular. I think because we did not think of ourselves as victims of circumstance, and that we did not talk a lot about Jordan and the major challenges we faced, most people simply did not think about it either. Our method of operation minimizes the challenges and focuses on the good. Although we never hid Jordan, some people forgot, or just never knew, what we were dealing with. One of my friends told me that another church leader said I should be doing more because my kids were older, and I enjoyed the services of household help. At that time Morgan was about 8, Blake 11, and Jordan 14. I thought, walk a little while in my shoes, lady, and then see if you still get miffed that I do not attend every event.

You need to prioritize your life. If you don't, someone else will, and that person's priorities will not necessarily be what is best for you and your family. Learn to say no, and ignore the fallout. Some people are your friend because they care about you, and you care about them. Some people are your friend because of what you can do for them. In other words, their motive seems to be, *I have so many ideas and goals, if you are not helping me accomplish my priorities, I do not have time for you.* That is not a real friendship. With some people, the best way to protect yourself from a deluge of requests is to love them from afar.

MY PRIORITIES ARE:

- God – Prayer, Bible, church
- Me – Nutrition, exercise, quiet time
- Husband – Communication, fun, alone time, sex, organized home

- Children – Communication, fun, advice when asked (this list would be longer if my children were not already adults)
- Business/Job – Exercise godly wisdom as my husband's business partner (I am no longer working as a church staff member, however, I am still a business owner with my husband)
- Friends/Extended Family – Mostly phone calls and lunches, some dinners and an occasional party in our home
- Volunteering – I serve, but I do not bite off more than I can chew — never again.

When I follow this plan, I stay happy. When I am happy, my whole family is happy. When I am not happy, they wish I would get happy fast.

Don't ever take your marriage for granted. You and your spouse have different needs and desires, gifts and talents, strengths and weaknesses, and usually a different personality. My husband is not shy, but he is reserved. He can be a chatter box if there is a conversation that interests him, but often he would rather do something else than talk. I can and will talk to most anyone. I start conversations with complete strangers. I am great at public relations. When I take (drag) my husband to political or business functions, he is usually not interested; he will hold up the wall. To him, it is a waste of time. To me, it is fun. I love connecting people to other people. Let's explore possibilities. Let's do lunch! It quite simply is not Paul's thing.

I appreciate my husband's qualities, as his perspective is often different from mine. When I stop and listen, I find wisdom. He is a meditator. I am not. I quickly make a decision, and off I go. My husband may draw me back, and we will have a discussion. I do not usually appreciate it at the time, but he is frequently right.

Value your marriage. It is unique to any other marriage. It is what you two have created together. Although I know he really can't, sometimes I think my husband can read my brain. He sees right through me. He seems to perceive my attitudes, good or bad, and he lets me know with a glance, *Deb, you are so full of it.* Or, *Perfect, you go girl!* Paul is my safe place. A place of total trust. Marriage is a living thing that will evolve over time, and keep growing. Work to maintain the love, the freshness, the passion —which is not always sex — in your precious relationship. The rewards are so worth it.

Chapter 6
GROWING OUR FAMILY

As Jordan grew, I knew that he would be a handful, but the love I felt for him made me long for another child. I saw how much fun my friends enjoyed with their children. I feared I might become a bitter old lady if I did not have a *normal* child.

I found it very difficult to see my friends' children passing milestones. It became a theme throughout Jordan's life for me. Johnny sat up today, Linda crawled...said his/her first word... walked...learned to tie his/her shoe.... As time marched on, those children Jordan's age got drivers licenses... graduated from high school... college...got engaged...got married...gave birth. I was always happy for them, but it became too painful for me. My friends' children would have been Jordan's friends, but Jordan would never truly grow up. Living with that reality became more and more challenging. I am sure I hurt my friends' feelings when I did not attend some weddings, bridal showers, and baby showers. It just hurt too much.

Paul and I talked about the risks of having another child. We never received an explanation about what happened to Jordan and no genetic problem that contributed to his mental or physical condition. The best explanation was no explanation at all. Could it happen again? Maybe, but *probably* not.

In addition to the built-in Jordan stressors, there were other considerations. In 1962 the Supreme Court abolished prayer in schools. In David Barton's book, *America: To Pray or Not to Pray*, (Aledo, TX: Speciality Research Associates, 1997), Barton reports in an effort to separate church and state, on June 25th, 1962 the U.S. Supreme Court ruled to abolish prayer in schools. Barton quotes a founding father, Noah Webster, who said, "No truth is more evident in my mind than that the Christian religion must be the basis of any government intended to secure the rights and privileges of a free people." In the long term aftermath of that crucial Supreme Court decision, the statistics are solemn regarding the decline of our society, especially affecting the family. Barton has many statistics in his book, but from 1962 to 1989 a decline of over 25 years showed and appears to be getting worse. Paul and I grew up in the LSD, sexual free-love era, and the violent years of the 60's; the extremely despised Vietnam War, numerous political assassinations, and the brutality of the civil rights movement. We have continued to experience decades of societal decline.

Could we raise great kids in such a negative, tumultuous world, especially with our Jordan? Our first-born was a surprise, but was it right to add another child, on purpose, with so much sin and violence in the world?

My job needed consideration. I loved working; I loved ministry. Could I handle it all? We really did not know at that time the full impact of what life with Jordan would bring. We could not, however, deny the yearning in our hearts to add to our family with another child. Was I going to allow challenging circumstances to make my decision, dictate my life? Not having my dream fulfilled would probably lead me to bitterness.

Maybe there is something you want to do. Do you want to go back to college? Do you want to travel? You need to fulfill your dreams. Do not allow yourself to become a victim of circumstance. That gives Satan way too much power. It may not happen overnight, but defy circumstances and do not deny yourself.

After much discussion and prayer, when we made the decision to have another baby, I became pregnant quickly. Funny, how we avoided pregnancy for 15 years prior to Jordan, and then found how easily I could conceive. I walked through that pregnancy with no fear at all. I knew I could not handle another child with problems and so did God. It was a decision made and lived out by faith.

We totally enjoyed Blake. Friends asked me what type of *program* I would put him in for early childhood education and development. I told them I would not put him in any kind of program other than playing with him every moment I could. My little buddy. He did everything on time or ahead of time, which was so exciting, except potty training. When he was 5, I told him he could not go to kindergarten if he still needed a Pull-up. He was decidedly not impressed. I also bought big boy pants he could wear when he always used the toilet. Three children in diapers (ages 2, 5, and 8) lived in my house; Jordan was not potty trained until he was about 10, which as you know did not last. I finally decided if Blake did not get trained by the time he got married, it would be his wife's problem. He is now a grown man, potty trained, and he went to kindergarten on time.

It was a more serious decision to have a third child. I talked to a co-worker, a therapist, experienced with disabled adults. I wanted to know what the future may hold for our care of Jordan. He advised against having another child. He said it would be overwhelming to our family. However, the seed of another baby, already in my heart, grew stronger. Raising a normal developing child was such fun. I knew I wanted to do it again. Nearing 40, with time running out, I knew the longer we waited, the riskier the pregnancy would be. We wanted to still be young enough to have enough energy to raise another child, and I wanted a girl. I placed my request with God.

Paul and I watched a television special regarding orphans in Romania. With tears running down his face, Paul said, we need to get one of those babies. I researched adoption and found with our age and with the responsibility of Jordan, we might find it difficult to adopt. I ended up giving my research to another mother who adopted two of her children from Romania. We needed to have our next and final child the old-fashioned way.

As with Blake, I got pregnant right away. We kept the pregnancy secret. One thing I did not enjoy about pregnancy is that babies became the sole topic of conversation, in addition to answering the question of, "How is Jordan?" Mostly I appreciated everyone's concern, but sometimes I wanted to respond, *Still retarded, but thanks for asking.* I know, I can have a mean streak. During pregnancy I got tired of saying, I am doing fine, thanks, and, 20 more weeks, 19 more weeks, and so on. I was glad we made the decision to keep the secret for awhile because in my third month, I miscarried. Disappointed, I cried a little, but I was not as devastated as some of my friends who experienced that same loss. My lack of emotion concerned me to some degree. I wondered why, but realistically, a miscarriage is not the worst thing in my life.

With all the years of high stress, events that should have caused me distress became less emotional for me; I grew a little numb. In fact, when little Blake would fall and hurt himself, I hardly responded. Mostly I would say, "You're fine," without even moving or checking. Blake expressed anger about that at one time, and said I did not care enough for him to be concerned. He expressed the same confrontation to his dad. With all the trips taken to the emergency room with his brother, and all Jordan's blood and stitches, unless Blake gushed blood we hardly noticed his little injuries. When we realized we hurt his feelings, we changed and expressed more concern and sympathy.

Shortly after the miscarriage, I conceived again, and again kept my pregnancy secret for the same reasons stated before, not because I feared miscarriage. However, during the third month I started showing signs of another miscarriage and I got mad. I told God I would not go through this again. I told Him, if I lost this child, I would never try again. If His plan included a third child for Paul and me, this would be the one, so He better save its life. God and I have that kind of relationship. You can, too. He can take what you dish out, but I find myself apologizing to Him on a regular basis. He is very quick to forgive, or maybe He doesn't even remember our tantrums.

God did save that baby, and her daddy named her Morgan. I got my girl, the grand finale. Another child brought about by faith. What a treasure, what a joy. Like Blake, she too is now all grown up and I cannot imagine my life without her.

My counselor friend was right; it was overwhelming. As Jordan grew more fragile it became very difficult to balance all the needs of my family. Would I do it again? Yup, I would. There may be other legitimate reasons to do or not do something, but do not allow fear to keep you from doing something you really want to do. God will find a way. He is the way maker. Oh, how I treasure my children!

I watched an episode of *Dr. Phil*, about a family whose adult children carried a great deal of resentment at the way their parents gave an inordinate amount of attention to their sibling who was drug addicted. All financial and emotional resources heaped on this one child at the expense of the others. I did not want to ever receive that kind of confrontation from our two healthy children. The fact was Jordan required a great deal of time, energy, and money. I was concerned that Blake and Morgan would become affected in an unhealthy manner; resentful and bitter because they did not receive the attention that they, too, deserved. I did not want them to rebel away from our family, the church, or each other. I wanted to raise my healthy children to be normal in every way. A recent conversation with Blake let me know that he did actually feel ignored at times. I expressed my deep regret. Blake understood and sincerely believed we did our best, but the feeling remained. The conversation made me terribly sad.

Once set, we did everything we could do not to break a promise or change a plan due to a Jordan emergency. We did not want our children to resent their brother. We did not want them to think of Jordan as being more important. He was not, but his needs could be spectacular. During an emergency, more often than not, Dad took care of it. He would race home from work and meet me at the emergency room. My husband spent many, many nights in a hospital to make sure Jordan did not wake up alone. I usually went on with our plans with the other two for the day or evening. We kept the worry, fear, and doubt at bay. Of course, the other two were aware, but after we prayed, we went on with their activities. It could be hard for us, as parents, but critical for the well-being of our other kids. When on occasion, with no other apparent options, we broke a promise, our kids stayed very gracious and understanding. They loved their brother. Once in awhile we were all disappointed.

A friend of mine wrote a book called, *Raising Teens Hassle Free.* I have to admit I did not actually read the book. The title alone put me off. Kids are not hassle free. They come with a personality bent and behaviors all their own that can make a parent shake their head in frustration. Proverbs 22:15

says that foolishness is bound in the heart of a child. Paul and I were not so unrealistic as to think we would not encounter challenges in raising our other two children, but we determined that Jordan would not be an excuse they used for making poor choices. We experienced some absolutely unavoidable issues regarding Jordan that were not common to most households, but as much as possible, these issues would not be the defining measure of our family life. We absolutely would NOT become victims of circumstance. We were a happy, peaceful, fun, godly family who happened to have a disabled family member whom we loved.

Make good, well planned, on-purpose choices, in raising kids; don't go with your first reaction, unless that reaction is a godly choice. I decided I wanted to pick my children up from school, whenever possible. I wanted to hear the first rendition of how their day went; it was very important to me, a top priority. After hugs and kisses, I began to ask questions:

How was your day?

OK

What was OK about it?

I don't know.

Did anything good happen?

Yeah.

What happened that was good?

How did you do on your test? Did you like

the lunch Dad packed for you? Do you have homework? What should we do this weekend? <u>Get them talking.</u>

Today, my kids tease me because they eventually realized that their determined mom would get them talking. They say, "Mom just would not give up. She made us talk to her." Yes, I did! Do not let your children get away with one-word responses. It is important for them to get into the habit of talking, and sharing what they think and feel; expression of *self* is important. It helps them become healthy adults, and it also keeps the line of communication open in the critical teenage and young adult years.

Talk to them before they go to bed from the time they are babies; this becomes a habit, and as they grow into their teen years, it may be the only time they will *spill the beans* on what is going on in their hearts. If you wait until they are teenagers to start this, your efforts may be looked on with suspicion and will become frustrating for all. Kids *need* to talk.

When Blake reached the age of about 10 or 11, we got him a bed with a ladder. The mattress was on top, and a desk and drawers built underneath. He climbed a ladder to get to his bed. A strategic error on our part. We would go in to say goodnight as usual, and there was this barrier between us — the ladder. The strategy at the time: one or both of us would go in to say goodnight. If we perceived something our child needed to release, we would gradually sit on the bed, and maybe lie down with them as the conversation progressed. If an experience hurt his or her heart, we might eventually hold our child in our arms as the tears rolled. The new bed situation did not work, and junior high is a highly critical season. We kept the bed for a very short season then gave it away.

Today, my kids are talkers. They are pretty open and confide in us on a consistent basis. When they do this, you better keep your mouth shut. Do not share the confidences of your children or husband with anyone other than God. Seriously! I learned a great lesson once while getting advice from another mother on a challenge regarding Morgan with which I needed help. It was Morgan's private business. I wanted insight to help resolve it. I learned later that my friend's daughter overheard the conversation. This child took the information to school, and it became not only gossip, but highly inflated gossip. Morgan was mortified. I was horrified. I learned such a hard lesson. I apologized, she forgave. It is not a mistake I repeated.

One more comment on getting kids to talk. Blake, as an adult, has asked me to please stop trying to get him to talk. He is actually a great conversationalist, and we have amazing discussions on an array of issues, including his very personal thoughts and feelings. He trusts his parents' wisdom and seeks our opinion regularly. Old habits die hard, and sometimes he feels like I am drilling or interrogating him. I no longer need to know everything, and he is not hiding anything.

While still young, we made events out of simple things. Starbucks serves a drink that the kids liked, so after school before they learned to drive, we stopped and ordered our weekly Frappuccino Friday drink, they also campaigned for Mocha Monday. We would talk and laugh as we drank our special drinks and planned the weekend. We all needed time away from the stress of our situation, and we did that on a regular basis. It did not have to be expensive, but it did have to be fun. We all wanted to laugh. Dad generally just went along with whatever we decided to do. He has always been wonderful that way.

IF YOU BUILD IT, THEY WILL COME

The Word says in Luke 6:38 to give and it would be given back to us. We wanted a normal, happy, family environment in our home regardless of Jordan's medical, physical and mental challenges. How did we do that? We decided early on to make our home a kid friendly environment. We became *the* house for many friends and parties. We always held the class party at the end of the school year. Kids also came to study, watch a movie, or have a bon fire. They liked hanging out. With two refrigerators and a big freezer, we served lots of food. Sam's Club loved us.

Our house came with a sport court, complete with game nets, and a hoop. We frequently rolled up the plastic flooring, and Morgan and her friends roller skated. We bought inexpensive vinyl covered barrel chairs for the basement, which made making-out much harder, added a projector and movie screen that rolled out from the ceiling and voilà – a theater room. These days a big screen TV works, but the theater screen created a theater feel; we served popcorn.

When we purchased a trampoline, one of Blake's friends moved it near the second-floor deck; he climbed the rail and jumped off. That kid went flying down, bounced, and soared back up high! Spectacular and fun, yes! Safe, no!!! We dug the trampoline into the ground so it could not be moved.

During some landscaping, we cut down a few trees in the yard, and in the process we discovered several big rocks. We placed them in a circle and dug a hole. Voilà – a fire-pit.

Black plastic and a hose make a superb slip and slide. During the summer our yard got ruined, but grass grows back, right? We had baskets of balls of all sorts, and water guns (hint: think about the Salvation Army and Goodwill for supplies). Provide fun activities.

We also supervised, supervised, supervised. The kids knew we were always around. We *visited* the basement every 15-20 minutes during movie nights when they were younger teens. Other parents knew their children would be closely observed when they were at our house. We expected the house rules to be followed. We restricted access to the top floor, therefore no members of the opposite sex were allowed in bedrooms, and they were not allowed to close their bedroom door with anyone else inside. Boys and girls could not be alone together, no kissing, alcohol, smoking, drugs, or physical touch. We were watching! Once in awhile a rebel infiltrated. In that case my husband would call the offending party to the main floor and give a brief, but pointed lecture, "We want you to have fun, but you will keep your hands visible at all times. Is that understood?" We might have missed some hanky-panky, but I don't think we missed much. Frequently, we stayed up way, way after our bedtime in order to stay aware. We often asked another set of parents to stay with us to have more eyes (or keep us awake). Often, we invited the kids to go home long after the published end-hour of a party. Nice to know they had such fun they didn't want to leave.

One night, we closed up the house, everyone in their respective rooms. With all the good-night process accomplished, Paul and I assumed the house to be in lockdown for the night. At about 11:00 pm I heard music. Blake's band practiced in our basement (I would try to edit books with drums and electric guitars playing directly under my main floor office), but after a brief moment, I knew the band definitely did not play my son's heavy metal rock music (with, I must add, Christian lyrics).

This band played more of an 80's style. Through the window shades, I saw the sport court lights were turned on. I opened a shade and behold, I saw Blake run out of the basement with blankets and pillows headed to the sport court. There were a half dozen teenagers from neighboring houses laying on the court with blankets and pillows listening to the music that originated from a large rental party-house venue in the neighborhood. In addition, a police helicopter flew over the offending party-house telling the hosts to turn the music off.

I noticed from my bedroom window that two of the kids began moving out of the light of the sport court and into the dark. With that, I decided our dog, Tifa, should be taken out for a quick run. Through all this activity, Paul slept soundly. I woke him and briefed him on the unexpected activity. He too, decided Tifa needed a run. Tifa, however, needed convincing to go outside. Grudgingly, she obeyed. We invited our *guests* in for hot chocolate and popcorn—an impromptu party. That's how we rolled. Be flexible. If they feel welcome, they will come — and yes, you want them to come. Say *yes* way, way more than you say *no*.

At times, we needed grace with the kids' teachers. Occasionally, Jordan ate their homework. That excuse being truly viable, we made sure Blake and Morgan promptly rectified the situation. Once, my favorite aunt, Violet, asked if Jordan liked books, and I could truthfully say, he *consumes* them. I don't know if there was a dietary need or simply a behavioral issue, but he liked to eat paper. In an emergency, I would let the teachers know the situation in case one or the other would act out in school or be sad with their worry. Staying in communication remained critical. It didn't hurt that one of my dear friends, Dr. Natalie Ellington, was the school principal.

When they got older with activities and jobs, it became more challenging to get family time. We finally landed on a once-a-week family dinner. Occasionally, I cooked, but usually, we went out and caught up with each other. From time to time, we also went to a movie. The kids actually really enjoyed these nights.

Our kids enjoyed many, many benefits that most kids do not have because we could make travel a financial priority. We love traveling, and we took Blake and Morgan with us as often as possible. We take amazing vacations. Experienced travelers at a very young age, after 9/11 happened, they soon became experts at going through security without needing our assistance. That kind of adventure may be outside of many budgets, but you need to find a hobby or some type of adventure: the beach, camping, hiking, snorkeling, a monthly movie, board games, trips to the library, people over for dinner, to keep the *happy* in your lives.

Our kids still like to vacation with us, when they can. We make it pretty hard to resist because we go to tempting, fun places. We know this season may end as they get on with their own lives more and more, but we intend to ride this wave as long as it lasts. It is hard to say *no* to Hawaii, London, Venice, Paris….zip-lining, snorkeling, and hot-air ballooning. The Atlantis Resort in the Bahamas is fantastic. We might try parachuting next…might. As glorious as this sounds, the point is to have good mental health, regardless of the situation you may be dealing with; your kids need to be given as much opportunity, as possible, to have regular fun.

Jordan was always there, taking part as much as possible. Our children's friends were exposed to him; it was not usually a big deal. To my knowledge, Blake and Morgan did not get teased much about their brother, although some were curious, which was okay. A boy said something mean once, and Morgan tromped on his brand new white shoes. That boy really howled. I do not remember if she ever apologized. When Jordan died, many of Blake and Morgan's friends attended his memorial service.

Do everything you can to make your home kid-friendly. Make the environment fun. Do not allow the fact that you have a special needs child, a small home, a small yard, worn furniture, or whatever to create excuses; if the environment is friendly and if you, as a parent, are relaxed, the kids will come. If you do not act sad, your kids are likely not going to either. Do not make your disabled child, or whatever your situation is, a big excuse. You absolutely do not want your other children to become resentful. Be a happy, normal family who happens to have a special needs child. Raise normal happy children.

Chapter 7
FAITH, MEDICINE, ALTERNATIVES

Paul and I are people of faith. Prayer is our first line of action, but without medical intervention, Jordan probably would have died in early childhood. Even though we sought medical treatment for him, we still believe that we walked by faith. He was at death's door several times.

Although it was very apparent that Jordan's needs were great, other than the stroke, doctors never made a specific diagnosis. We believe he was somewhat autistic. His mental and physical challenges could not have been simply from the stroke. People who have strokes young usually go on to live very normal lives. While there may be some residual effects, depending on the size of the stroke and where it took place, other parts of the brain take over, especially in a child where the brain is still developing. Jordan's progression and development were more than slow or delayed.

After birth, Jordan came home from the hospital on a medication called phenobarbital to help control his seizures. The simplest explanation of a seizure is that an abnormal electrical type of charge happens in the brain resulting in loss of control of both awareness and body movements. People will usually drop to the ground while the body flails out of control. There are several types of seizures, and it is often hard to describe and differentiate one from the other. People with epilepsy have seizures, and often the cause of the condition is unknown. Jordan's stroke caused a brain injury that resulted in the seizure disorder. They are not the same condition, but the appearance and treatment are the same. Neurological experts will likely cringe at my explanation.

What I didn't know at the time is that Jordan's medication can make a person extremely grumpy. So as a very inexperienced new mom, I did not know why what comes naturally to humans to comfort a child did not work on Jordan. I saw other mothers picking up their children when they cried and the child would be comforted. Jordan cried no matter what I did. My insecurities as a mother increased dramatically.

Even on the drug, Jordan continued to have dramatic grand mal and other types of seizures. Out of all of his major challenges, the seizures were the worst. Sometimes more of one kind of seizure, sometimes more of another kind; all of them awful. One particular type of seizure was especially painful for his dad and me to hear. It usually took place with Jordan in his crib, so there was no fear of falling. During this particular kind of seizure, he screamed. When he first started having them, we would fly to his crib, and realized they occurred in his sleep. It sounded like a horrible nightmare; like he was in terror, lasting anywhere from 30 seconds to a minute, but each one felt like an hour. Eventually, gratefully, he grew out of those.

In hopes of a solution for the seizures, Jordan's neurologist prescribed several medications, and when those didn't work, more medications, and when those didn't work, a different combination of medications. Jordan became little more than a zombie. His personality and body were drugged all the time, and any seizure improvement did not last long.

OPTIONS

This chapter will do a lot of weaving. I tried to organize my information, but as you read, you will find I could not. Bear with me. You might find a treatment that is exactly what your child or loved one needs. I hope you do. Please don't be afraid to try different treatments. Western medicine is not all there is.

I began to think out-of-the-box. I wondered if there might be something else available, other than drugs, for seizure control. I began searching for alternative treatments. It was quite the journey. We found improvement with some of the treatments, always very exciting, but most did not work for Jordan, or the success was temporary. I learned some treatments worked for some people, but not for others.

One of the first treatments we found was through the National Association of Child Development (NACD). The origin is a program called the Institutes for the Achievement of Human Potential, and was developed in Philadelphia by two men named Doman and Delacato. Glenn Doman wrote a book entitled, *What To Do About Your Brain Injured Child*, published by Doubleday in 1974. A relative of Dr. Doman, named Bob Doman, ran NACD, taking the program across the country. A holistic approach, it encompassed physical therapy, nutrition, and educational input. This program required dozens of volunteers. I will never fully know what we accomplished with all of the exposure to therapy and educational pursuits, but we followed the protocol of this program for well over a year. During this time Jordan finally began to walk.

Other alternative treatments included: massage, acupressure, acupuncture, chiropractic care, Botox, cranial sacral manipulation, naturopathic care, nutritional supplements, live cell injections derived from sheep, and Chinese herbs, among other treatments. Jordan's seizures were still not controlled.

The Chinese herbalist is a funny story. I know Chinese medicine has its roots in ancient history. Sometimes we westerners do not have knowledge or respect of some forms of medicine and often we (and western doctors) are closed to different medical approaches. I, however, searched for answers. I made an appointment with a Chinese herbalist at Bastyr College, now known as Bastyr University located in Bothell, WA, north of Seattle. During the appointment, the herbalist examined Jordan and began to make his recommendations. He could speak English, but his accent was very heavy, and understanding him was difficult. He asked me if I had any fresh deer antler. I thought I misunderstood him, "Excuse me, do I have any what?" He asked again, "Do you have deer antler? Fresh best, dried okay." I about choked. I told him I did not have any deer antler, fresh or dried, except those ancient antlers that hung on the side of Paul's family cabin on Whidbey Island, WA. He said he could get me some. And he did. He made some kind of a concoction and instructed me to make a tea out of it. I actually gave that completely unknown substance, other than the deer antler, to my child. So vile and nasty tasting, it took me hours to get it down him. That particular treatment in alternative medicine did not last long.

The acupuncture was interesting. Jordan seemed to enjoy it, but I do not know if it helped him. After many, many months of acupuncture, on one visit I needed to use the bathroom so I wandered around the office looking for one. I encountered a very large Buddha. I saw crystals placed around the office. I knew about New Age, but I decided to ignore what they represented. I don't believe in such things, and I just decided to appreciate them as being pretty rocks. I could not, however, get past the Buddha. We never went back.

I found Botox injections fascinating. Our health insurance actually paid for them—surprise! Our insurance did not usually cover alternative treatments. Jordan received two injections in his left hand; the goal was to loosen his hand, which he held extremely tight, part of the paralysis from the stroke. The injections worked for a season. We went to town on exercising that little hand to get it loose, but when the Botox worked its way through his system, the tightness returned. We could not pay for the injections without insurance coverage.

Regarding insurance, it is unbelievable what insurance will and will not cover. Jordan wore a helmet to protect his head should he have a seizure. In addition to a hard-shell helmet, he wore a face guard and chin strap. When I approached our insurance company, Group Health Corporation, about covering the head-gear, they would not cover his helmets. They would rather do surgery on a broken head than help prevent an injury with a protective helmet.

One particularly challenging treatment we tried was live cell therapy injections. The cells were derived from sheep, the treatment intended to help Jordan's brain heal. My simplistic rendition of the theory is that when the live cells were assimilated in his system the damaged part of his brain would grow normal cells that would possibly enable him to walk more normally, maybe help his left hand relax, and possibly help the seizures. The moral issue of live cells challenged me. I finally decided God gave us animals for our use to meet our needs. Usually, people would think of wool or meat being derived from a lamb as normal and acceptable. Well, what I needed were the live cells from the sheep.

The cell therapy provided lasting help with Jordan's walking. He began to cross pattern walk up the stairs. Cross pattern is when one uses alternate legs for each new step up a staircase as opposed to using both legs to get up one stair at a time. He also walked on his left foot incorrectly and developed his muscles in a way that caused him to walk on the side of his foot instead of the flat bottom of his foot. This therapy totally changed that. Jordan actually noticed the difference, and that was a pleasure to see. He stomped up each stair correctly, like a personal victory each time he did it.

We continued to have tremendous challenges with the seizures. I wish I knew then about the potential benefits of marijuana oil for seizure control. Some families have experienced exciting benefits in their children with seizure disorders and epilepsy. I am quite certain, given the chance, we would have used it for him.

When Jordan was about ten, Paul and I saw a program on television about a diet that kept kids from having seizures. It is called the Ketogenic Diet. The program was administered out of Johns Hopkins Medical Center in Baltimore, MD. I contacted the administrator of the program and was told that they did not accept patients outside their area. I was not ready to give up on the idea and ordered their book to learn more about the Ketogenic Diet. The diet is highly controlled, very complex, precise and specific. It is very heavy in fat, and very low on carbohydrates. The plan was fascinating, and I wanted to see how it might work. I convinced Jordan's neurologist into getting me an appointment with a dietitian to discuss this possibility. The dietitian consulted with Jordan's pediatrician, and she consulted with his neurologist. They reluctantly agreed to put him on the diet.

The patient starts the diet with a fast and Jordan's physicians insisted that he be hospitalized for the fasting portion of the diet. When food is given every meal has to be precisely measured by weight. I knew from reading the book that the diet was extremely specific and difficult to administrate, but if this diet really controlled seizures, I was more than willing to test it. Based on what I read, I knew the first day he was given food following his fast that the dietitian was not knowledgeable enough about the diet for it to be successful. She was not specific enough in the foods and brands she selected. The diet not only requires certain foods (not just cream, but cream with a specific fat content), and measurements to the gram, it also requires some specific brand names to meet the criteria (not just hot dogs, but Hebrew National hot dogs). The hospital did not follow the diet as precisely as the book said the program required. Ultimately, the diet failed.

As a side note, I read labels to know the actual ingredients in food items. It proved challenging. A quart of one brand of heavy cream contained a different amount of fat than the pint of the same brand. I called the dairy to see which was correct. They could not believe how fussy I was being, and it became a war of words. I found another brand.

Still not willing to give up on what might be a miracle waiting to happen, I again contacted Johns Hopkins Medical Center. Impressed with my tenacity and persistence, Jordan became the first out-of-area patient for the Ketogenic diet program at Johns Hopkins. Within weeks we flew to Baltimore. Jordan was on the diet for approximately two years. It worked and reduced Jordan's seizures to almost nothing. When his body chemistry began to change as he grew, the diet could no longer control the seizures as well. As I recall, the diet is not meant to be forever in the strictest form. Eventually, the diet is to be modified, and the brain is supposed to cooperate. Jordan's did not. When we stopped the diet, the seizures returned with gusto.

VISITING THE PRESIDENT'S HOUSE

I am including the following experience so you can remember to keep yourself open for adventure, even in the midst of trials. One hysterical story came out of that diet. We were scheduled to return to Johns Hopkins for a second visit. About two weeks before we left, Paul drove to work one day and saw a man standing by his car on the side of the freeway. Paul never stopped to pick up anyone before, but the gentleman was well-dressed, driving a new car, and for some reason this time he did.

It turned out that the man was an agent for the secret service; an advance man for President Bill Clinton. The President would visit a local community college to give a speech. This man came to Seattle in advance of the President to coordinate and oversee how the President would get through the crowds, which buildings he would enter, which doors to go through, and where the security team's sharpshooters would be located. Every detail is mapped out, coordinated, and communicated. It is impressive.

The rental car this man drove broke down; he was on a tight schedule and needed help. Paul took him to a car rental agency, and while the man was thanking Paul he invited us to visit the White House for a private tour if ever we came to Washington, D.C. Paul replied, "Don't mess with me if you're kidding, because we just happen to be going to Baltimore in a couple of weeks."

We made arrangements to meet in the Old Executive Office Building, across the street from the White House. As we met the man at security, Jordan, in his wheelchair (which we used on occasion), did not feel his best, and just flung his arms, hitting the guy in his private parts. Nice first impression. As we entered his office, Jordan, still being a little agitated, flung his arms again and cleared the guy's desk off; papers went everywhere. You could see the pleasure die in the man's eyes.

As we walked into the White House, there were a few stairs, so we needed to use the elevator — the President's elevator — to get to the main floor. Upon entering, Jordan, who loved buttons, pushed a few, including the emergency button — you know the sound. When the elevator door opened, there were at least four men with hands on what we assume were holstered guns, looking for the bad guys (terrorists?), who invaded the White House — wow, us? By this time our guide must be really regretting his invitation.

We went through the Roosevelt Room and the Oval Office, and all the while Jordan was repeatedly making a sound (one of his old favorites) that he considered really funny. He put his fingers in his mouth and made a retching sound, the sound you would make just as you are going to heave into the toilet. He did this over, and over, and over again, and laughed every time. He thought he was hysterical, and on occasion he actually was successful in his retching, leaving a prize; you know the kind I am talking about. It made us very nervous...the possibility of vomit on the Oval Office carpet, which gratefully did not occur. I was pretty embarrassed by the entire episode, and I was ready to leave Jordan in the Press Room, permanently.

When we finally got out of there, we, and I am sure he, was glad our visit was over. Doesn't it make a great story, though?

A DIFFICULT DECISION

It finally became apparent that all the medication and alternative treatments could not control the seizures. Some of the things we did for him paid off physically and perhaps helped in his educational development, but the seizures were literally killing him. We discussed a hemispherectomy sometime in the past and dismissed it as too radical, something we did not want to do. After exhausting all other possibilities for treatment, it became our final viable option. His window of opportunity was closing as he neared the age of 12. By that age, the brain is not as easy to retrain. It was a gut-wrenching decision, surreal.

A hemispherectomy is where a neurosurgeon essentially cuts the brain in half, allowing the damaged brain portion to simply die in the head. The theory is the healthy side of the brain will take over much of the function of the damaged side of the brain. The hope is that the damaged side of the brain will stop causing seizures, and the healthy side of the brain would not have any.

Following the surgery, Jordan spent several days in the hospital. Doctors tested some of his functions, his eyes, the strength of his limbs, and he seemed to be okay. When you operate on the brain, there is always a chance that some functions can be damaged. We did notice that he did not drink his fluids. Since the Ketogenic diet was no longer a concern, we allowed him to be given the opportunity to drink juice and pop to see if we could spark his interest in drinking.

Even though drinking continued to be an issue, they released him to come home. Over the next several days, things went from bad to worse. The surgical side of his brain began to swell up, and he seemed to be even more lethargic than right after surgery. We called the surgeon who treated

us like overly nervous parents. Our experience
with brain surgery was indeed limited, but this did
not seem normal. When the swelling on the side
of his brain ruptured and fluid came pouring out,
we returned to the hospital. Jordan required more
surgery to close up a hole that the surgeon left
in his skull that allowed brain fluid to leak out.
A couple we know, Roy and Ethel Anderson, she
being a neurological nurse, stayed one night with
Jordan in his room, allowing us to go home for a
much needed night of sleep.

During this time, my sister, Julie, who adored
Jordan, also came to stay with him in the hospital,
and she spent Thanksgiving Day with him. It
enabled Paul and me to spend a (sort of) normal day
with Blake and Morgan. I know of another hospital
time when we feared we might lose Jordan, and
she visited him alone late one night. My sister is a
mortician, and she knew she would be taking care
of him after he died. She wanted to see him once
again to hug and kiss him, and to say good-bye
while still alive.

When we returned home from the hospital,
things did not improve. Jordan continued to be
lethargic, yet somehow he retained his very sweet
sense of humor. Nearly comatose when I finally
called his doctor late one evening, he advised me
to take him to the hospital. They did some tests
and determined that his sodium count was 197.
A normal sodium count is between 135 and 145.

My understanding is that people can begin to decline dramatically when their sodium count is in the 150's. Jordan was transferred to Children's Orthopedic Hospital in Seattle, WA, and was admitted to intensive care. Doctors came to his room just to look at him because they never saw a sodium count of 197 in a living human being. I wish I could find his discharge papers because a medical professional would find this hard to believe. During this time, I wondered how much worse hell could be than this.

Eventually released from the hospital, Jordan went to a type of rehabilitation center for disabled children, called Ashley House, a remarkable place with qualified, caring people. Jordan hated it. We were asked to stay away for a bit so he could adjust to his new environment. When I did visit him, his eyes begged me to take him home. He followed me to the door when I left and he waved good-bye to the staff, like he, too, was leaving. Being afraid to take him home and deal with the full responsibility of his new needs, I ultimately could not leave him there. Jordan wanted to be at home. I called my husband and let him know what I decided. He thought the same thing.

Doctors determined that during the brain surgery his surgeon severely damaged some glands in the center of Jordan's brain. His seizures greatly reduced, but from then on until his death we battled the effects of those damaged glands.

Amongst other challenges, Jordan could not control his body temperature effectively. We found that if he actually did have a normal body temperature, his body responded like he was sick and began to have seizures. Since his body temperature was now naturally low, whenever he was hospitalized, which was regularly, the nursing staff, as part of their protocol, tried to warm him up with large heating pads. That brought on major seizures.

We began putting large signs up in his hospital room giving the medical staff instruction, and sometimes lectures, on not using heating pads on Jordan and why. Sometimes I would enter his room and find the heating pads on him; once I pitched a fit, yelled, and threw the pads on the floor shouting, "Can't you read the signs, *No Heating Pads*?" Not my finest moments. I knew his healthcare professionals tried to do their best, following protocol, but we knew Jordan so intimately. We could often see on his face what he could not say himself.

Early in this adventure, I would agree with whatever doctors said, but they really are *practicing* medicine. I learned to speak my mind, ask questions, and I challenged their perceived authority. From their frowns, scrunched up faces and eyes that would not meet mine, some of the doctors and nurses appeared less than happy to see me. I would not win a popularity contest. As Jordan's advocate, I did not care. Today, I am a very outspoken person (my family and any of my friends who read this will agree, *Oh, yes, she is*).

One of the greatest challenges we dealt with was a condition called *diabetes insipidus.* It is not related to sugar diabetes. Some people call it water diabetes. Do you remember when I told you that Jordan did not want to drink fluids following surgery? An indication of this condition is being repelled by fluid. We monitored his fluid intake precisely, similar to the food in the ketogenic diet. After several years of trial and error, we finally settled upon 16 ounces of water plus whatever amount of fluid he consumed in food. If we deviated from that plan, he would have high sodium or low sodium, both of which are life-threatening.

Since Jordan did not want to drink fluid, his doctors decided it would be a good idea to put a feeding tube in him, this would enable us to get water into him easily. We were reluctant, but ultimately agreed to the procedure. The tube didn't last long. Jordan didn't like it, and he made it his purpose in life to open up the little hatch in his stomach and yank on it. The ultimate result was he pulled enough to damage the tube rendering it unusable. It is very stressful to try to get a child, who really did not understand why, to drink his water. We made it a game. It took him years to really cooperate, but eventually he would drink his water willingly in exchange for tortilla chips (or other chip-type snacks). What a little champ.

Eventually, we became aware that Jordan's growth was stunted; a result from the damage made to his brain during surgery. He began to appear odd. His full height would not become more than 5'2". His beard growth and appearance was of a man in a little kids body. He no longer appeared normal and the sparkle in his eyes was often gone.

MORE CHALLENGES

One time, Jordan simply stopped eating. He did not act sick; he just did not want to eat. That was highly unusual because Jordan was a chowhound. We took him to the doctor, who couldn't find anything wrong with him, but because he would not eat we went to the hospital where they took numerous tests and finally determined that his appendix needed to be removed. By the time they drew their conclusion, it had ruptured. Some of his medication disguised the test results that determined an appendicitis problem.

Paul usually spent nights with Jordan in the hospital. He can sleep anywhere (on long flights I get very envious). We never wanted Jordan to wake up alone and be afraid, and we also knew that he could be uncooperative in the presence of strangers, especially strangers who tried to touch him or hurt him with needles. This one time we were exhausted, and we could see the hospital was well-equipped, with an amazingly compassionate staff. Jordan being very well sedated, we went home. We warned the staff that with the exception of a few phrases, Jordan was nonverbal; they should not expect a response when they talked to him.

The next morning when we arrived back at the hospital, the nurses met us with almost an accusation in their attitude and tone of voice. They said, "You told us Jordan couldn't talk, but he can!" We asked them what he said. They said when they walked into his room that morning Jordan said, " Who are you?" So they explained to him who they were. Then, Jordan said, "What do you want?" Paul and I got a great laugh out of that because those were two of Jordan's phrases. He said them randomly, for no reason at all, but on this particular occasion, he used them appropriately.

While essentially non-verbal, Jordan tried hard to get his wishes known, and we tried hard to understand and meet his needs. Often it remained a mystery, and from time to time we would apologize for not comprehending what he wanted, making a suggestion of something else he might like to do. Sometimes he would just look at us with resignation in his eyes. How sad that was to me.

Arranging to go on vacation was challenging! Before having a full-time caregiver, my sister Julie stayed with Jordan occasionally. That was a tremendous blessing. One time, Paul and I got into a car on the way to the airport as Jordan's caregiver, Rhonda, began to help him to the nanny mobile (a van for our caregiver's use), when he fell and broke his arm. She could have stopped us before we drove off, but she knew how we desperately needed the break, so she handled the situation herself. We did not know until we returned. Isn't that amazing?

As the years went by, Jordan developed other chronic conditions. He got pancreatitis on a regular basis, and he developed a swallowing disorder that caused him to aspirate, giving him bacterial pneumonia. His doctors talked to us about reinserting a feeding tube to get Jordan his nutrients and withhold food by mouth, but we knew Jordan would not accept it, being a chowhound. He loved food. Even if it meant shortening his life, we would continue giving him food. His aspirations mostly took place during sleep when he did not swallow saliva correctly, or when he vomited during illness. It also could happen during a seizure. Eating was not really the problem. His doctor agreed that withholding food would be a terrible punishment for Jordan and hell for us. I could see us doing swan dives in the air to rescue him from putting food in his mouth. Jordan was becoming increasingly difficult to care for, but we loved him so much.

Paul and I used both faith and medicine to keep Jordan alive. A scripture we learned a few years ago is, *He who is loose and slack in his work is brother to him who is a destroyer and he who does not use his endeavors to heal himself is brother to him who commits suicide* (Proverbs 18:9 Amp). We never gave up, but we accepted what we could not change, a real balancing act. I believe there may have been a few people who believed we compromised our faith by using medical professionals and medicine, but my response is: walk a mile, or a year, or a decade in my shoes, then tell me your perspective. If you can do a better job, please, be my guest.

Some people complimented us on how we handled our son. They would say things like, "I could not do that. I guess God knows who is and is not capable of parenting a developmentally disabled or sick child." We would say, "Thank you," but I would think, *maybe I missed the OUT button.* I did not feel strong or capable. I played the cards I was dealt to the best of my ability. Once a dear friend told me how much she respected us for the way we lived our lives. She said, "You really did have a choice, Debbie. Other options could have been utilized for Jordan. You could have sent him to a home for people with developmental challenges." Yes, we could probably have chosen a different road, but as I recounted the conversation to my husband, he said, "For us there is no other option." I agreed.

My prayer is that some of our experiences and our search for options will help you as you pursue potential answers to your loved-ones needs. Don't accept status quo. Get out of the box.

Another way to do something positive is to advocate for legislation to provoke change. Most of what you see in accommodations for the disabled originated from parents or loved ones. Someone has to be the squeaky wheel, like my brief, but effective fight for a designated bathroom in Jordan's class. Do not stop advocating for what your loved one needs. You can do this.

Chapter 8
JORDAN'S VICTORY

Jordan received his healing on Friday, March 18, 2011, at 9:22 am when he died at 25 years old.

Three years prior in March 2008, Jordan developed another bout with bacterial pneumonia due to a seizure and his swallowing disorder. The doctors did everything they could, and we decided to take him home to die. We brought our other children into the decision-making process, along with a few trusted friends. We wanted Blake (19) and Morgan (16) to understand the choice. We did not want them to have unasked or unanswered questions about what would happen. With funeral arrangements made, documents signed, Jordan went home to hospice care with a hospital bed, oxygen, morphine, and other equipment. Paul and I took Blake and Morgan with us to a counseling session. We wanted to be sure we were all as prepared as possible for Jordan's death, but, Jordan surprised us. Every day he got a little stronger, and by the third day, he ate pizza. We spent the next three years on gifted time with him.

In June of 2010, Jordan fell and broke his hip; it was so surprising to have that happen. He was just walking along with support from his caregiver, Rhonda, and boom, down he went. During surgery, the orthopedist placed a metal rod on his hip bone and restricted him from walking for three months. We feared that might be the summer from hell, but in reality he did not want to walk due to the pain. We wondered if he might refuse to walk ever again.

A few days short of three months following surgery, Rhonda, busy with something, could not get to Jordan just as soon as he called for her (remember, while non-verbal, Jordan could make his wishes known, for the most part). Patience was not one of Jordan's outstanding virtues, so when she did not arrive as promptly as he wanted, he decided to get up and walk on his own holding on to furniture and walls. He smiled like he was pretty clever, but Jordan never really walked well on his own again. He was afraid. From then on, his mobility became very limited, and his life more sedentary. I believe he needed more exercise to help keep his lungs clear. The broken hip was the beginning of the end. He went into a downward spiral of illness and weakness, but he still kept his humor and smile.

In early March 2011, Rhonda called and told us Jordan's breathing was not right. Battling a cold, Jordan produced excess phlegm, but when we saw him we knew it — pneumonia again. We immediately took him to the hospital. By this time the admitting staff knew Jordan on sight, knew his history, and could see his distress. He was admitted to urgent care. Before the end of the evening, he moved to intensive care and was intubated. He spent a week on the respirator as numerous tests and procedures were implemented, in addition to being given antibiotics.

Jordan showed signs of improvement. They kept reducing the oxygen as his need for it declined. Removed from the respirator on Monday, March 14th, he breathed on his own. Paul helped reassure Jordan, and immediately as the respirator came out, Jordan said a husky, but loud, "Daddy!" Such a pleasure to hear; everyone smiled, and some shed a few tears. I asked the nurse when he would be able to come home? If he continued to hold his own ability to breathe, the nurse estimated that it might be on Thursday, which would be March 17th. I slept so well that night.

On Tuesday the 15th, I spent some wonderful hours with him. We played *Jordan games*, which consisted of butterfly kisses with our eyes, sticking our tongues out at each other, playing with his fingers and kissing his hands, tickling his feet, and other little activities. He was not at all interested in his videos, books or puzzles. One of Jordan's hands was mostly paralyzed from his stroke, but for some reason he wanted me to play with it. Whenever I stopped, he would push his hand toward me. This was unusual because that hand was sensitive. It was a high compliment when he allowed anyone to touch it. I consider that day playing together to be a special gift. As the day went on, I could see the beginning of labored breathing, again. It was not a good sign.

On Wednesday morning the 16th, Paul and I met with the doctor, and he told us we had reached the end. Everything possible had been done. He could be intubated again, but that would only buy us a few days at most, and since the procedure is so traumatizing, it did not seem like the right thing to do. Not assimilating his fluids and nutrients effectively, essentially his body was already breaking down.

Paul and I knew in our hearts that this day would eventually arrive. I cried and spent some time with Jordan while he was still conscious. As soon as we said our good-byes the hospital staff was going to sedate him as his lack of ability to breathe caused him some distress. I brought Morgan to see him for the last time. Blake was out of town on a tour with his band.

I knew I could not watch Jordan die. I worked so hard and prayed so much for his healing. Letting him go was a terrible gut wrenching decision. To watch him die would be too awful. Paul, however, chose to be with him but did not fault me for not wanting to be there. Jordan was transferred to Rhonda's home for his final hours. She loved Jordan as her own, having been his caregiver for 16 years.

Deciding to let Jordan go was crushingly painful, but not hard. I know that may sound odd, but love allowed us to make the right decision for our child. Living it out was excruciating, surreal. The last nine months being so very difficult for him, we did not want our baby to suffer anymore. Jordan actually did get to go home on Thursday, as the nurse predicted, but this time to die. There was no doubt — we knew we would not get our miracle of extra years this time.

Jordan went home on a full measure of oxygen and sedation, by ambulance; all other medications were withdrawn, including fluid and nutrients. My faith switched gears, and I prayed that my beloved boy would not suffer at all in his final hours, and he didn't. My concern that he would panic as his lungs filled with fluid, and he could no longer breathe, never happened. Hospice made sure his sedation covered him very well.

A few visitors came on Thursday. Hardly able to respond to them, he managed to indicate he knew of their presence. A special person came to visit, Darla, a friend of Rhonda's. Jordan really liked her and could say her name, but this time, she got a fling of his arm as proof of his awareness.

Paul spent a lot of time with him on Thursday. He told Jordan it was okay to go to be with Jesus.

Paul told him we loved him and that we would see him again someday. He stroked Jordan and cuddled with him. Touch is such a miraculous way to comfort. Paul and Jordan's relationship was sweet, tender, close and precious.

Rhonda laid Jordan's feet on her thigh during the wee hours of Friday morning and rubbed them. She said they felt hot. Whenever she stopped, he put pressure on her thigh indicating he wanted more.

On Friday morning, Jordan's eyes opened. Rhonda believes he was looking into Heaven. Sometime around 9:00 AM that morning, his breathing changed. I think he hovered between Heaven and earth. She called our house and let Paul know, who had returned home for a very few hours of sleep. Who could sleep, really? He left immediately. Rhonda told Jordan that Daddy was on the way. If he wanted to go to Heaven it was okay, but Daddy would be with him soon to say good-bye. Rhonda lived a few minutes away, and Paul arrived in time to kiss Jordan, tell him we loved him and he would soon see Jesus. With that, our beautiful, treasured son was gone. Paul was with Jordan for his first breath and for his last.

Paul left to come home to tell me. Our Morgan arrived home, too. She had actually gone to school that morning. I think she was robotic. She could see the pain on her daddy's face and she knew. Paul and Morgan entered the house together. I asked if Jordan was gone; my husband nodded, yes. We hugged each other and cried. Shortly thereafter, Paul returned to Jordan's body.

We could not announce Jordan's death to anyone until Blake knew. Out of town on tour with his band, we did not want anyone to send him a text or talk about it on social media, neither did we want to tell him ourselves over the phone; it was too impersonal. We called the parents of a band member, who instructed their son to gently tell Blake, knowing he was surrounded by good friends. With that assurance, we started communicating with our other family and friends.

The night before he died, Paul went to Jordan's closet and picked out an outfit. He carefully ironed the clothes and took them to Rhonda's. Paul took off Jordan's hospital attire, washed him and changed him into his clothing. He and Rhonda waited for the mortician to arrive, who just happened to be Jordan's aunt, my sister Julie.

I am so grateful that my sister is a mortician. I knew she would treat Jordan with love and care. She adored him. She said she talked and sang to him all the way to the funeral home. I made up special, personalized songs and sang them to him over the years. Julie knew them all. Yes, she is a Christian and no, she did not really believe he could hear her.

Earlier in this book, I talked about the importance of having friends. Jordan's memorial was the ultimate example of friendship. My method of operation in a crisis is always to go into action. When I knew Jordan was dying, I asked a friend, Chris Cook, who works in the media department at church, to make a video of Jordan's pictures. I gathered most of the pictures three years prior when we feared Jordan would soon be leaving us. Chris dropped everything and created a beautiful photo memorial to use at Jordan's service.

One phone call to our friend, Terry Schurman, and Jordan's memorial service planning went into full swing. The rooms at the church were booked, the time set, food volunteered for a meal following the service; Paul and I met with Terry briefly and then with a few short phone calls to and from my sister, the service was planned. Between Julie and Terry's incredible coordination, Paul and I made very few decisions.

The service itself was perfect. I would not change a thing. We did not want anything lengthy, so it lasted about an hour. Casey, our friend, and pastor was in town and able to clear his schedule to act as master of ceremonies. Rhonda's pastor also spoke, along with two of our friends, and Julie. We sang one song, *Amazing Grace*. It was perfect. We laughed, we cried, we mourned, and we celebrated, shocked that several hundred people attended. Very nice — very generous.

Rhonda's brother, Kevin, suggested we ask for books in lieu of flowers, to be donated to homeless shelters and children's hospitals, a wonderful idea knowing Jordan's penchant for books. We received well over 500 children's books. We placed stickers on each of them with Jordan's name and photo as a memorial.

The weeks and months following Jordan's death were very, very hard. One day, in prayer, I felt God ask me if I could ask for Jordan back, would I? I knew, in reality, I could not get him back, but I told God, no, I would not ask for him back. I missed him terribly, but I knew where Jordan lived. As his mother, would I ever do anything deliberately to hurt my child? I would not. I know that Jordan is in Paradise, in a beautiful new body, living as a man for the first time in his life. He is no longer a child in a man's crippled body. He is no longer ill or in pain. He is normal.

Today, Jordan is healed, strong, and whole, going about his Father's business. He has a job in Heaven and is productive. Would I ask for him to return to earth? Never! That said, I still miss him. For over 25 years, Jordan entered my mind first thing in the morning and the last at night, but he does not need me anymore, and I am still working on not needing him. It makes it a little easier for me to think of him as attending *Heaven University*, and he cannot come home for a visit because it is too far away.

It is not natural to bury your child. You plan to bury your parents, maybe a sibling, and eventually you or your spouse will go, but our children are supposed to outlive us. With Jordan, his death is a mixed blessing. Concerned about his life after our deaths, we made both financial and guardianship plans for him, but as I wrote earlier, he began to be increasingly difficult to care for. We wondered if, upon our deaths, he would be too much of a burden for anyone, and would need to be institutionalized. With his fragile health, we did not think anyone outside the family, with the exception of Rhonda and Greg, could comprehend his needs. We often instructed his healthcare providers on what and what not to do. Such a complex critter. We were afraid, outside our immediate care, he would suffer.

I kept waiting for relief to kick in as time went on following his death. There was no longer any worry. Certainly his expenses were gone. We know where he is, and that he is being cared for and loved by our heavenly Father. One would think I would be breathing a sigh of relief; I am not. I still miss him and wish I could touch him. Of course, I know I will see him again one day. Heaven has become more precious to me. I want to enjoy what earth has to offer, my beautiful living children and my sweet husband, but I am excited about Heaven. It truly does bring me comfort knowing Jordan is there. Praise the Lord!

In the next chapter, you will learn about mourning. I felt God work in me every passing day. As I look at it now, from the perspective of having gone through most of it, I recognize every day was a pinch better. While it may feel like it, at the time, your life is not over.

Chapter 9
MOURNING

When someone dies, part of the healing process for those who remain is remembering the good times, the fun experiences, and the benefits that loved one gave to this world through his or her life. In a sense, Jordan died at birth, the person he should have become, a loss of who and what he was meant to be. I believe that God provides opportunity or benefit in every situation, and came to realize that Jordan's life was not a loss; he did serve a purpose.

Around the occasion of Jordan's birthday following his death, I knew I needed to get some closure for myself. It became apparent it was not going to come with time alone. I started this process of closure by writing a list of the benefits of having a disabled child. There really were some benefits. With every benefit I recognized, the devil took a hit. The Word says in John 10:10 that the devil wants to steal, kill, and destroy — chaos, death, destruction, is his whole purpose — but God brings life.

Here are some of the ways I turned a negative

into a positive by changing my thinking. What the devil does for evil, God uses for good.

1. Jordan automatically became a citizen in God's kingdom. Usually, people think that the age of accountability is about 12. I suppose that is a good measure, but in reality, some kids (especially when they've been raised in the church) are accountable much earlier, others never exposed to church, maybe a little bit later. Jordan would always be a child, not accountable, sinless. He will spend eternity with our heavenly Father, with a new and glorious body — pain-free.

2. If Jordan had been normal, my other two children, Blake and Morgan, might never have been born. I did not desire children in the first place, and I likely would have been very satisfied with just one child. I loved working full-time in ministry and after adjusting to the idea of having a child, I felt that I could continue to do so with only one, but as much as I loved Jordan, I felt such a tremendous sense of loss all the time. Jordan, though such a darling, would never develop normally. As much fun as I experienced with him, in spite of the difficulty, it made me long for another child to love. When Blake was born, well, what an absolute blast; everything went easy with him. I decided I wanted a girl, and— ta da — not quite, but very soon thereafter came Morgan. God gave me the desires of my heart. So there are two more

citizens of God's kingdom, who will serve Him all their lives.

3. My other children, not immune to the difficulty of living with a disabled brother, endured Jordan's version of socialization, which could be gross and embarrassing in public. His behavior could be bizarre (example: sometimes he would lick people's skin or clothing, or spit). They have been frustrated and angry with their brother, and at the same time, they felt guilty or sad because they knew he did not understand and could not help who and what he was. They became offended when others treated Jordan disrespectfully. So... what is the benefit? My surviving children have compassion and a sweetness about them toward people who are different. Those traits will always be positive features in their lives and an asset to others.

The list goes on, including this book, but the point is, I purposed in my heart that what Satan intended as loss for our family, I would find what God has used for good. Has it been difficult? Yes, absolutely. But ultimately I win, and I like to win!

Prior to Jordan, I experienced the death of a loved one. My step-father, who I loved and who in many ways became my dad, died. Paul's parents, both gone. As I write this, my biological father is nearing the end of his life. The death of my child took me way, way beyond any level of grief I ever experienced. I honestly wasn't prepared for the crushing sadness. The finality of death is profound.

After Jordan's memorial, I closed his estate. Primarily that meant that I let the state of Washington know that Jordan William Willis died. He owned no earthly possessions of value, but still a mountain of paperwork needed to be filled out, followed by the ever so challenging appearance in court to stand before the judge. The finality was so clinical. I called different government agencies to let them know that Jordan would no longer require their services or benefits. Paperwork, paperwork. I resented it.

I wrote dozens and dozens of thank-you notes; hundreds of donations of books were acknowledged and distributed to various charities and hospitals. We gave away Jordan's very well-loved videos, books, puzzles, and clothes to non-profit organizations. Everything got sorted, packed up, and delivered, everything finalized and accomplished; with nothing more to do for him, no other way to serve him, he was gone, and my job — over. I no longer had three children; I had two.

I kept Jordan's pictures around the house just as they were prior to his death. In fact, I added a very large photograph of him to a wall in our bedroom. I have wondered at the wisdom of it, as sometimes when I look at it, I cry. At other times, it warms my heart. As different experiences have occurred and life has gone on, some of his pictures have been replaced with more current events. I did not want to make a shrine.

I kept up on all my volunteer activities, meetings, and appointments. Many advised us not to make any changes in the first year, but I felt detached from everything, from life. I talked and smiled at all the right places, but I finally knew I needed to drop a few boards and committees. I went through the motions, not really contributing. I decided if I could not be a fully engaged board member or committee chair, I needed to step down. I knew I could not coordinate the major projects my positions required. My family believed I would be sad that I no longer held high positions. Instead, I felt relieved. I know eventually that there will be a time when I will want to take on another project. Sometime...

I smiled and accepted, with as much dignity as I could muster, people's expressions of sympathy. Many praised us for our care of Jordan over 25 years. Sometimes, however, we humans say stupid things. One woman said it must be easier for me to lose Jordan since I sort of already knew he would die before me anyway. That left me speechless. I have found, unless you are a super close friend, the best thing to say is, "I am sorry for your loss." Those who said simple things like, "I am so sorry you lost your Jordan," or, "I will miss his incredible smile," we appreciated. Anything more than that I could not handle, especially in public. When you keep your expression of sympathy simple, without asking questions, it leaves the grieving person free to talk a little more about how they feel or to simply say, "thanks."

When people asked how we were, I felt uncomfortable, put on the spot, like I was being tested. Sometimes I wanted to say, *I feel like crap and I want to cry. I could barely pull myself out of bed this morning, if you want to know God's honest truth.* My usual response became, "We are doing fine. Thank you for asking." Rather than asking a grieving person how they are, a better thing to say is, I am so glad to see you or you look good today, even if it is a little bit of stretching the truth. The grieving person will get your message.

One very sincere friend once said that we blazed a trail for our group of friends when we chose to keep Jordan at home and raise a successful family. After Jordan's death he said, *Now, you will blaze another trail and show us how to grieve terrible loss.* I knew he meant it as a compliment, but, wow, I felt tremendous pressure to perform. What if I did it wrong and led someone astray?

On my first Mother's Day after Jordan died, I received extra special hugs and sympathetic smiles from people whose names I did not know. As church leaders, a lot of people know us, but we do not know them. I think, for the most part, those folks lost children of their own and could understand what we were going through. It might have made them feel better, but it did not help me.

My goal those first few months... get to church and get through a service. The greatest challenge? Being in public made it convenient for people to express their sympathy when they saw us. At times, if it was a bad morning, I would not go to church at all. I did not want to talk to anyone... a really bad choice. Sometimes I went, but sat in the back, so I could make a late entrance and a hasty retreat. I wanted to feel normal, and church is normal. Maybe I could have handled it better. I don't really know if there is an actual right or wrong way, but at that time, I did my best.

I did not sob in public, but I often found myself springing leaks. My daughter and I began referring to those times as *having a moment*. Anything could bring it on. I knew, hard as I tried, that I was not myself, and those close to me could tell I was not all right; they would acknowledge *my moment* with a smile, and we moved on. My friends knew I did not want a lot of sympathetic attention.

The first Christmas following Jordan's death, I had to decide if I should include a photo of him on the card. I knew some distant people might not know of his death. I honestly did not want to receive cards addressed to our family that included Jordan's name. I decided to send our cards out very early with a brief message about our loss and a picture of him. It might not have been the *merriest* thing to do, but I think it may have saved me some pain. I also knew it would be the last card I would ever send that included Jordan.

A few months after Jordan's death someone asked me why I still mourned. She felt the need to explain to me that Jordan went to Heaven, and was living with Father God, healed and whole, happy and safe. I asked if she would not miss her son if he died? She said that "Yes, I would, but my son is normal." I realized that she considered Jordan to have been a problem, and that through death, the problem was now resolved. I wanted to poke her in the nose.

It is true, my relationship with my son was somewhat different than the one she has with hers, but love has no boundaries. My love, the deep love of a mother is the same as hers, and I miss my child; I am not at all relieved that he died, but I am happy for him.

Even though I walked through the motions of life, I felt depressed, feeling like an imposition on my family when I talked about my sadness. I certainly did not want to be a detriment to their healing. Our children felt sad at moments, but generally were doing fine, and actually so was Paul, for the most part. He became concerned about me and we went to visit a couple; both are friends as well as trained therapists, Roy and Ethel Anderson (the people who spent the night at the hospital with

Jordan after surgery).

We all talked at length, and I expressed my dismay that I was so troubled. Jordan had lived on grace for a long time. What our friends said shocked me. They said I had developed PTSD (post traumatic stress disorder). Wasn't that a condition for returning veterans who experienced the unfathomable horrors of war? In reality, many, many people experience this condition as a result of something traumatic, like a car accident, rape, other physical trauma, maybe a natural disaster, or like me, the death of a loved one.

I cared for Jordan for 25 years through terrible challenges, hurts, disappointments, and trauma; busy taking care of him, and carrying on my other responsibilities with all diligence. During those years, I did not take time to take care of me. In reality, there was no time to take care of me. I could not just drop out of my life and pick it up again somewhere down the road, once I felt better. The subsequent letdown – Jordan's death – following that kind of intense responsibility would take time to heal.

They said not to feel guilty if I did not want to return to work, wanted to drop volunteering, or wanted to stop or start whatever; there were no rules to follow other than to take care of me. Now, in reality, I still had a husband, children (albeit almost grown), and home responsibilities (what's for dinner, Mom?), but I understood what they meant; Debbie needed to take care of Debbie. I felt such freedom, especially knowing my husband agreed. He wanted me to be happy and healthy. Paul actually made it clear to our children. He explained, Mom needs a break. What did that mean? It meant anything my husband and I wanted it to mean. What a gift.

Paul took Blake to Beijing a few years earlier. When our daughter graduated from high school a few months after Jordan's death, she wanted a trip alone with Dad, too. They went to Italy, the last place on Morgan's bucket list she wanted to see before she turned 21. She had already traveled to New York, Washington, DC, London, and Paris. During the time they would be gone, Blake would be on tour with his band, *A Hope Not Forgotten*. I decided this would be the ideal time to get some chapters done on this book. Not a good idea. Even though I found the constant interruptions from my family to be somewhat irritating when I wrote, I found out I needed the interruptions. I got way too depressed when I wrote for extended periods of time on such a painful topic. I decided not to write when I would be alone for an extended period.

One day while writing a particularly painful section of this book, I stopped typing and began to sob, truly in an abyss of grief. Blake came up behind me and started patting me on the back. His effort to comfort me was touching, and I appreciated it, but I misinterpreted his action. He said, "Mom, you need to move away from the computer to do that. Your tears are wetting the keyboard. You are going to ruin it." That struck me so funny I started laughing like a crazy woman. Blake, not sure what to do with me, just stood there looking helpless. My family keeps me in the real world. They bring me joy. I need them.

I wondered at one point if my husband still grieved. It bothered me that he might have moved on quicker than I, so I asked if he ever felt sad. He said, "I kissed Jordan's picture before I left work today." He also admitted that he does not think of Jordan as often as he once did. I know everyone expresses grief in different ways at different times. There is no right or wrong.

A therapist from hospice came to my home one day at my request. I invited Rhonda to be with me. I knew she, too, mourned deeply with me. At one point I said, I just want the grief to be over. I want the pain to go away. I am a Christian woman. I am a woman of faith. I will see my boy again. I know where my child is, and I am happy for him (as I cried). The therapist showed me a wheel of the grieving process. It is not an orderly list. A person who is grieving goes through every step, but in no particular order. There is also no specific time you stay in that place. Frankly, I wanted to just skip the grieving process altogether, but if one resists and fights it, one will simply prolong it.

One area may be quite easy to get through. Anger, for example. If I was angry following Jordan's death, I did not recognize it. I experienced anger when Jordan was first born, but I do not recall it when he died. In some ways, I had mourned Jordan since the day he was born.

Mourning encompassed every part of my being. For example, things that usually interested me, no longer held my interest. I felt exhausted all the time. One might over or under eat. One might become a frantic *doer* to keep busy. One might withdraw. You can anticipate to a degree that you will behave in a certain way, like in childbirth; I knew I would not be a screamer, and I wasn't. Following Jordan's death, I cried, certainly, but I was not dramatic; no fainting, no screaming, no dropping to my knees, but there laid a deep, deep, sadness inside me.

There is a saying we have in Seattle (maybe other places say this, too): if you don't like the weather in Seattle, wait five minutes, and it will change. That was me. I could be fine one moment, but in the next my eyes would fill with tears.

I still lived in the same house, with the same husband, same church, same friends, same car. The mail needed to be retrieved, we needed to buy milk, and the newspaper still arrived every morning. Paul, Blake, and Morgan, were where they should be, but with Jordan missing nothing felt right. I didn't like thinking people would be judging me, but I pretty much knew people watched us. I felt on display. How is she _really_ doing?

There are books written about the steps to mourning, but as the hospice therapist suggested, I think of the steps to grieving as a circle rather than a list. You may visit places in the circle very briefly, some for a longer period, and some places you may visit more than once. For example, if you find someone made a medical error that caused the death of your loved one, you may very quickly bounce back to shock, then anger again. You may visit more than one _place_ at a time. The reality is there are no solid rules, but you should not deny what you are thinking and feeling. People who have not gone through a tremendous loss may feel after a few months, you should just _get over it_, but really, maybe they just _don't get it_. I am not advocating intense grief year after year, but for at least a brief period, and probably longer, you will highly likely experience intense feelings. If you do not grieve, you might be in denial.

The following should not be considered an _official_ list. These _places to visit_ following the loss of a loved one are based on my personal experience and the experiences of others in my circle following the death of a loved one:

1. <u>Shock and/or Denial and/or Numbness.</u>

During the initial time of loss, the shock, denial and numbness can actually help one to not be overwhelmed. Even though we knew Jordan was gone, the reality of our loss felt surreal. This may be one of the times in life where someone else may need to stand in the gap for you (Ezekiel 22:30) spiritually. Your faith might be challenged. God understands our human emotions.

2. <u>Pain and/or Guilt.</u> Life may feel almost unbearable, tortured, a feeling of overwhelming suffering or pain. You might feel remorse for something you perceive you did or did not do. If you could change something, you would, but you can't. Even if you find you cannot pray, the Holy Spirit is there to comfort you. He is always there.

3. <u>Anger and/or Helplessness and/or Blame.</u> You may feel a sense of frustration to downright fury. Lashing out at someone is not productive and can damage all but the strongest of relationships. Words can cause scars in humans, but not with God. Don't keep your feelings inside, but release them to God or at least a person who is not as emotionally involved. A feeling of helplessness or hopelessness can zap you of all your inner resources, but your loved one cannot come back, and death cannot be fixed. Talk it out.

4. <u>Depression and/or Loneliness.</u> None of these stages felt fun, but for me, this became the worst and the longest. After a few months, I felt pressured by some that I should move on. I

heard things like, "This is not like you, Debbie; you are stronger than this; this committee **really** needs your support," and more. I appreciated that for some it was a sincere expression of love and concern or need. For others, I made *them* feel uncomfortable because I was clearly not myself. My usual outspoken, take charge personality was no longer evident. After a few months, the full measure of my loss became apparent to me. I felt empty, removed from life, and not able to pull myself out of it. Still going through the motions, my heart was not in living my life. This was about the time we visited our friends, the Anderson's, who started me on the road to recovery.

5. <u>Acceptance and/or Hope and/or Happiness.</u> Even though you may not want it to, life really does move on. You begin to emerge. Life is calmer. Your emotional load is a little lighter. As your mind begins to clear, you feel a little more functional. The practicalities of daily life force you to begin to focus. Accepting the undeniable does not mean that you instantly become happy — although you may, but for most, it is still a process. You will never be the same, but you can still feel the joy of life. You are developing a new normal. The wonderful healing power of God works in everyone, Christian or non-Christian. Frankly, I believe one must fight hard to stay sad. Peace and happiness just sort of bubbles up in spite of ourselves. Even when you do not want to leave your beloved in the past, you

are propelled forward by the joy that life brings. The gut wrenching pain will grow weaker in time. You will feel anticipation. Life will bring happiness again. Thoughts of your beloved will not be as painful, and memories will be sweet (although your eyes might still fill a bit). My empathy for others is greater, and I find I am more emotional sometimes, as I can identify with their pain.

Some people stay stuck in a sad place for a long time. I do not think that is particularly healthy. If that happens, the grieving person might need some help getting out of it through therapy. I knew a woman actively grieving over the loss of her child who died during childbirth. She spoke of that baby often. From her level of grief, I believed her loss to be recent. It actually took place three years prior. One never forgets, but she needed help getting over that hump to move forward.

In the 23rd Psalm, the Bible talks about walking through the *Valley of the Shadow of Death*. I think of that valley as a real place in our spirit and our mind. Hard times come, but God does not want us to live in that valley. It is not a place for the living. It is a place of death. God wants us to walk through that place. He does not want us to live there; it is temporary. Don't fill out a change-of-address card and stay. John 14:26 in the Amplified version of the Bible says the Holy Spirit is our Comforter, which means our Counselor, Intercessor, Advocate,

Strengthener, and Standby. God made a *get out of jail free* card for us to use. So, use it. I do not want to feel sad. I want to feel happy. My life is blessed. I will see my son again someday. I have a wonderful life to live here and now. I want to experience it all.

Jordan is still so real in my mind. I still can hear his sounds and see his smile in my memory. Rhonda always used a certain clothing detergent and a certain shampoo on Jordan. When I smell it on someone, Jordan flashes across my mind and heart. I can still feel his hair in my memory; it was very thick and it grew like a weed. I loved rubbing his head and he loved having me do it. Sometimes those kinds of thoughts bring tears to my eyes, but I have discovered that I can miss my son and still be happy.

In my future, there are weddings, grandchildren, and travel. I do not know what other plans God has in store for me. I am sure whatever it is, it will not be something I expect. God has a great sense of humor in that way. I love God. Patsy Cameneti, one of my favorite teachers, has said, "Don't you just want to thank God for God?" I do.

FACTS VS. TRUTH

Everyone has challenges, disappointments, tests, and trials. You don't get through this life without them. But don't allow circumstances to destroy you. Determine to follow God's Word.

There are the *facts*, and there is the *truth* about

your situation. *Facts* do not determine the course of life, but *truth* does. The *fact* is my child died. He was mentally disabled, physically handicapped, and medically fragile. The *truth* is God is able. Self-pity and being a victim are not part of God's plan for my life or yours. The *truth* is, there is a way. Whatever you need there is a way to live in peace.

In order to overcome difficult situations, you must know, understand, and renew your mind to God's Word, and then stand strong for as long as it takes. Don't look at your circumstances, the *what if* and the *why*, and feel robbed, angry, or bitter. That won't help. Look at the truth, which is the Word. When you understand the character of God, the overwhelming love of God, and the compassion of God toward you as His child, you gain confidence.

I have a wonderful family and a happy life. My children are mature Christians even though they are still young adults. We have defied the odds. Many people in our situation have very sad results from the stress of the years of challenges. We have fought for happiness. We are blessed.

God has a plan for you and His plan for you is good. My life changed, but my destiny has not. The road to destiny is not straight. There are hills and valleys, turns and detours, but when you take control of your mind, and understand God's Word, you can overcome anything. Choose to overcome!

Chapter 10
AS THE YEARS GO BY

A YEAR LATER

The original title of this book was *Overcoming Difficult Situations*. Blake read this manuscript one day and said, "You know, Mom, we never really *overcame* with Jordan. He did not receive his healing on earth. What we did was successfully live through a lot of years of difficulty. It was more like a journey, and we lived <u>through</u> the difficult situations." Thus the title of the book changed. What is most important to me is that my family not only survived, but we thrived both during and after Jordan's life.

Eleven months after Jordan's death, my father died. He became the sixth death in my family in a period of about 14 months. Jordan was the fourth. I found my reaction to Daddy's death to be much different than that from my son's. The pain and sadness were simply not there. We expect to bury our parents. It is the order of things. Perhaps it was just too much, too soon after Jordan, but my dad's death was not the worst thing I ever experienced. Although there are many his age who are healthy and still going strong (including my mother), at 80 years old my father lived his life. My most precious memory of his relationship with Jordan was watching my dad feed my son chocolates. They made a mess, but it seemed to give Daddy great pleasure and brought smiles and chuckles to them both. I sadly rejoiced in my father's passing as he was very much ready to go, and I know I will see him again.

Our beloved son is gone. Who could have known as we started planning our trip to Italy that our precious treasure would be in Heaven when the trip actually took place. Jordan is with his Lord and Savior, and how happy he must be now, healthy and strong. Every special occasion, including Jordan's birthday, has been lived through without him. The pain of his loss is not as acute now, but I do not think I will ever stop missing him. Love grows with the birth of every child; it is not divided, so everyone gets a smaller share. Love for another person does not die upon the death of that person. I love Jordan today as much or more than the day of his birth. Even with the Comforter, who is the Holy Spirit, and the knowing beyond doubt where my son is, the sadness of not having him in my daily life took me beyond anything I ever experienced. I can still easily weep today if I think about it too long.

I once considered it odd when people would say that someone *passed away* or *passed on*. It seemed just another way to say that someone died, but in a less blunt manner. There really is, however, a difference. I know that Jordan's body died. His earth suit is gone, but Jordan (as we all are) is a spirit being. Jordan's spirit is very much alive. Even though our bodies die, our spirits *pass on* to Heaven (or hell). Jordan is just living in a different, Heavenly realm. It is a wonderful, beautiful place and I will see my boy and others I love when I get there. In the meantime, I will remember...

If you are at all concerned about your eternal life, you need to get right with God and make Jesus the Lord of your life, to know you will live in Heaven when your life on earth is over. Our spirit-lives go on forever. When your earthly life is over, you are going to go somewhere. Where will you spend eternity? Visit www.christianfaithcenter. org; there you will find information that will help you make the most critical, most important decision of your life.

My prayer is that this book will serve a purpose in your life. I hope the information will help you to successfully live through challenges or difficulties, and that you will not allow circumstances to control you. As I end this book and this chapter in my life, I am happy to move on to what lies ahead.

I will never forget, and I will always love and miss my beloved boy, but life goes on, and so must we.

FIVE YEARS LATER

I thought I was done writing this book, but it just never felt finished. Around the fifth year following Jordan's death, I realized why; I needed to heal more and tell you about it. It truly does get better. I still think of Jordan nearly every day, especially just before the anniversaries of his death and birthday. I love him every bit as much as I did while he was alive. My family and I still talk about him from time to time. Remember when...? Most memories we talk about are the ones that evolved into funny ones. I think the best way I can explain it is the pain softens and what is left behind is a scar. My friend, Wendy was hit by a car decades ago. Her injury has long since healed, but there is still a scar. It is a reminder of her experience, but she does not dwell on it.

I always want Jordan's life to serve a purpose, to use our experience to help others. I have had the opportunity to pray with other parents who are in the midst of pain from a recent loss. Some who don't know our story have said, "You could not possibly understand." Ah, but I do. Once a lady sought me out to pray with her because her dog just died, and she thought I could identify with her loss. I wanted to laugh, but I didn't.

I was asked to write a small entry about our experience for a book. Pastor Treat included our testimony from the pulpit during a church service, a series entitled, *God, where are you?* I have been video recorded talking about Jordan for broadcast within the church. Recently I was interviewed by Pastor Treat for our television program. Hard? Yes. Worth the pain? Absolutely.

I could hardly fathom getting to this place in my heart and mind five years ago, even though it was my goal. I am happy; I am at peace. Our life story is still being written. I do not know the future or God's plan for our family; weddings, grandchildren, travel, and... what? Jordan is in Heaven doing his work and waiting for us. I am still very much looking forward to seeing him, hugging him and talking to him, but I am not in a rush. With the perspective of eternity, as Wendy would say, "Earth life is short, but Heaven life is long."

Morgan has graduated from college (a very happy day). She started her first professional job in her field shortly after graduation. Blake works full time and is also a full-time student, finishing college. He still loves music, loves photography, and is a very busy guy. No marriages, yet, and I am happy to say, they pay their own bills. Hallelujah!

Do not allow the pain of your past to rob you of the joy in your future. Open your eyes, open your heart, look for the good, the positive, the fulfilling. I promise it is still there.

Message from Jordan's dad: HE WAS MY SON

My wife, Debbie, has already expressed most of what I want to say, but I have a few additional thoughts. Jordan led a very simple life, but his needs were great. I miss his smile, his little limp, rolling on the floor with him, hearing him chuckle, and his cuddles. I miss his laugh, his little naughtiness, his vocalizations, and expressions. I do not miss his frequent blood draws, the seizures, the numerous doctor visits, the emergency room, and his toileting accidents. Jordan was content with very little, yet he taught me so much — how to love unconditionally. He was my son. I love Jordan as much as I love Blake and Morgan. My love for him is still with me today. Although very different from his siblings, his value is equal. I miss him greatly.

Message from Jordan's brother:
AN EXPERIENCE OF A LIFETIME

My name is Blake Willis, and as I write this, I am 22 years old. I am Jordan's younger brother, and up until writing this, I never referred to myself as such. I never really functioned as Jordan's younger brother. Living with Jordan — definitely an experience to say the least— but as odd as it may sound, now that he is gone, I wouldn't change a thing. Of course, at times, I wished my brother was normal, but I wouldn't have learned some characteristics and life lessons if things were *normal*.

For a long time, I resented God for the way Jordan developed. I wondered how can God, the guy who created our entire universe, let something like this happen? I prayed that Jordan would miraculously be healed, but it never happened. Towards the last years of his life, my prayers changed from, *God heal him* to *God, just take him*. I really didn't know what to pray for anymore. I don't know why Jordan could not be normal, and I don't know why God didn't heal him while he was alive. I do know that God didn't make Jordan mentally handicapped.

If anything, God made Jordan a part of our lives because, with us, he was able to live a very good life for someone in his situation. We loved him, and he received the best care possible.

If it wasn't for my parent's financial success, I'm not sure what would have happened to Jordan had he been born into another family. I wouldn't wish Jordan on anyone else. I know I will see my big brother in Heaven when my time comes. Jordan taught me a lot without saying anything. I have patience, am slow to anger, and have a lot of compassion. I try to be more understanding with people because I know not everyone is quick to catch on.

It's hard sometimes to know he is not here, and I do cry from time to time. My parents are brave and have definitely blazed a trail, setting an example for others. I'm happy they are my parents, and I am happy that I had the privilege of knowing and living with my brother.

I knew Jordan was sick before I left to go on tour with my band, *A Hope Not Forgotten*. Jordan nearly died before, so I already had faced the possibility of his death. I had a feeling this would be his last time with us. My parents never wanted us to make adjustments according to Jordan's needs; they wanted us to simply live our lives. The night before Jordan passed away, we played a show in Fresno, CA, and the next day we would be in San Diego. We wanted to get further south early so we could walk around Hollywood. We ended up driving through the night, and I slept miserably.

We stopped at a Denny's at about five in the morning and slept a bit in their parking lot. We ate breakfast at eight. Getting ready to leave, my friend, Morgan, pulled me aside and told me Jordan passed away. My parents did not want me to receive the information over a phone call. My parents called Morgan's parents and asked them to call their son; they knew we were together. I became visibly upset, but I also felt relief, like a burden had been lifted. Jordan was healed, although not in the way I preferred him to be. The band members were so great, too. They knew the situation, and they held me and made me feel comfortable. They didn't have to say anything.

"He's in a better place," people would say. That didn't make me feel better. Just because I knew where he went didn't make the situation easier. The fact is that he isn't here on earth anymore with my family and me. There were some benefits with Jordan's passing; in fact, a lot of benefits came out of it. Jordan's expenses stopped, so my parents no longer had to be concerned about that, or the need to set money aside for a trust fund to support him in the future. There were no more emergency trips to the hospital or frequent trips to the doctor. There were no more medical bills. My sister and I did not have to babysit, we did not need to clean up after him, but when a person is gone, those things that you do for that person seem so much more valuable and are such a small sacrifice.

When I am in Heaven, I believe I will see him again. I believe we will actually get to talk to each other. Until then, a part of Jordan lives on through me. The qualities he has instilled in me, unintentionally mind you, will help guide me in how I treat others, and ultimately in how I live. I don't always think of Jordan anymore, but living life with him has allowed opportunities for me to empathize with people going through the same situation. We are the sum of our experiences, and Jordan will forever be with me.

Message from Jordan's sister:
HELPING OTHERS THROUGH JORDAN

I am Morgan and as I write this, I am 20 years old. A week after the one year anniversary of Jordan's death, my brother, Blake, and I were on our way to join our parents and grandmother in Italy. My mother gave us the rough draft of the manuscript for this book to read. She said she wanted us to know what she wrote and wanted our perspective. She did not necessarily want us to read it on the flight, but that's what we did. Hard to read, both Blake and I cried. The flight attendant looked at us with concern several times. Reading brought back all the memories and feelings. Some of what we read was new to us because it happened before our births or when we were very small.

Since Jordan had always been a part of my life, I knew nothing different. It was not until junior high that I realized not everyone had a Jordan. Instead of feeling upset or ashamed, I felt proud; he was a sweet person who I loved. I still do. My parents always wanted us to feel free to have our friends over and encouraged us to fill the house.

Everyone just got accustomed to him and his weird ways. I did not enjoy all the work, everything about helping to meet his needs, but I loved him very much. I miss him. Jordan died when I was a senior in high school. It took effort to enjoy the fun things of graduation. Jordan's timing was awful, but my parents, as usual, did not want Jordan's needs to ruin anything, even his death.

After my parents had made the hard decision to let Jordan go, I went to the hospital to say good-bye. It was not the first time. Jordan nearly died before, but I knew this was the last time. It was surreal to realize I would not see him again for a very long time. His life on earth was over. It was all just really hard.

One thing that is important to my parents is that they want Jordan's life to serve a purpose. They somehow want to help others through our experience. That opportunity came my way. About a year and a half after Jordan died, the younger brother of one of my girlfriends died in an unexpected hiking accident, a shocking tragedy. He attended church that morning and then he, his older brother, and friends went hiking. He and one of the others slipped, fell, and died that afternoon. Thousands attended their joint funerals. In California, the day my friend's brother died, I felt pretty helpless. When I returned home, I visited with her briefly. I took her my favorite brand of tissue. I have a lot of experience with tissue. I knew she would need me more later on when some of the shock wore off.

A few weeks after the funeral, my friend called; we met for coffee and talked. Everything I stored up from my experience with my brother came pouring out. I could put into words what my friend felt. It helped her. She said, "I understand now why you were the way you were in school." I was never one to participate in all the drama teenagers seem to attract. I had real drama at home. Actually, I criticized the behavior of my classmates. They seemed to come up with excuses to make up drama, and it bugged me.

A person is a person no matter how small (Dr. Seuss). I love this quote, and I believe it. Everyone serves a purpose. I believe that in life you can make an impact in somebody else's life. You might think your testimony, your opinion, does not count. The hard things that you go through in life, and what God pulls you out of and guides you through make you a stronger person. That's your testimony. You might not know why you're going through it or why this bad thing is happening to you, but you also do not know who it is going to affect in the present or your future. Your testimony can help people and yourself. You really can do it. I thought I was alone, but God was there the whole time.

acknowledgements

Many, many heartfelt thanks go to so many people: To my former assistant, Debra Popejoy, and my friend Terry Schurman for giving the script the first critical reads; I felt safe giving it to you. To Terry, too, for Adventure Fridays and making some very hard days easier; adding Richard, along with Doug and Cindy Ostrom, for helping Paul and me make an impossible decision. To Randy Lagerquist for sitting quietly with us for hours during Jordan's brain surgery. I am grateful beyond words to Casey and Wendy Treat for saying *yes* to anything I needed. To Darlene Anderson for helping to organize Jordan's exercise program, absolutely beyond my coping ability at the time, and to the dozens of volunteers who put down their work with great attitudes to help him. To Joel and Tracy Smith, and Susie and Tom Gauthier for staying in our home as we took a break. To Monica Anderson Croonquist for your help and for diving down the stairs to save Jordan from a fall; you can hardly see the scar. To Jill Thompson for making Jordan's meals for his Ketogenic diet; he never liked bacon or hot dogs again. To Mary Anderson for caring for my kids and my home while I escaped to work. To our nanny, caregiver and friend, Rhonda Berg Jones, who loved and cared for Jordan, Blake, and Morgan as your own, and mourned Jordan's death as much as we did; your husband, Greg, and your whole family are stars in our eyes. To Dr. Kenneth Wheelock for caring for Jordan, Blake, and Morgan without charge, and Dr. Patrick Fleege for generously taking Jordan on as his dentist. To Carol Swanson and Theresa Fazekas for your many years of generous friendship. To Annie Elder for being such a kind and giving person. To Sheri Blumberg and Kim Wesolek for final proofreading and to Lisa Garrison for your interior and book cover design, photo, and patience. To Roy and Ethel Anderson, whose counsel started Paul and me on a long path to healing, and to Kristy Ziemke for therapeutic, listening ears. To Chris Cook for producing a wonderful video of Jordan's life; to date, I have not watched the memorial service, and to his sweet wife, Shelley, along with Carmen Goers for political distractions. To Dr. Natalie Ellington and the staff at Christian Faith School for generous compassion and understanding. To my mother, Clineene Smith and sisters, Susan Schwalb and Julie Hartman for their love and support; Jordan could make family events *interesting*. To Molly Venzke, author of *Caged*, who helped me make this book better, and I actually found some of it fun! Finally, a huge hug and thanks to my son, Blake for being nit-picky and focused on editing. There are others who had a part in Jordan's life and ours that I surely have missed, and my family thanks you.

With few exceptions, these people are part of our church, Christian Faith Center. Get into a church, develop relationships, and stay there! Amen.

Made in the USA
Middletown, DE
24 May 2021